HOUGHTON MIFFLIN

MATH
Expressions
Common Core

Dr. Karen C. Fuson

GRADE

5

Volume 1

This material is based upon work supported by the
National Science Foundation
under Grant Numbers
ESI-9816320, REC-9806020, and RED-935373.

Any opinions, findings, and conclusions, or recommendations expressed in this material
are those of the author and do not necessarily reflect the views of the National Science Foundation.

HOUGHTON MIFFLIN HARCOURT

Cover Credit: (Cheetah) ©Stephen Meese/Alamy

Printed in the U.S.A.

ISBN: 978-0-547-82425-3

11 12 13 14 15   1689   21 20 19 18 17 16 15 14

4500477312   B C D E F G

Use the fraction bar below for Exercises 1–4.

1. Label the first part of this fraction bar with the correct unit fraction.

2. Circle the first four parts of the bar. What fraction of the whole does this circled portion represent?

   _____

3. Write your fraction from Exercise 2 as a sum of unit fractions.

   _____

4. Represent the whole as the sum of the unit fractions.

   _____

5. Solve the problem below by circling parts of the fraction bar. Write the appropriate equation below the bar.

   Brett is building a fence around his yard. He has worked on it for two weeks so far. He finished $\frac{2}{8}$ the first week and $\frac{3}{8}$ the second week. What fraction of the entire fence has he built?

   _____

   Eighths

6. Nena thinks that because $4 < 6$, it must also be true that $\frac{1}{4} < \frac{1}{6}$. Explain to Nena why this is incorrect.

   _____

   _____

   _____

   _____

Name _____   **Date** _____

Remembering

List all the factors of each number.

1. 16 _____   2. 29 _____

3. 33 _____   4. 40 _____

List the first four multiples of each number.

5. 6 _____   6. 11 _____

7. 15 _____   8. 1 _____

Complete.

9. $\frac{1}{3} + \frac{1}{3} =$ _____

10. $\frac{2}{7} + \frac{3}{7} =$ _____

11. $\frac{6}{10} - \frac{5}{10} =$ _____

12. $\frac{4}{6} + \frac{2}{6} =$ _____

13. $\frac{4}{9} - \frac{2}{9} =$ _____

14. $\frac{1}{10} + \frac{1}{10} + \frac{1}{10} =$ _____

Write an equation. Then solve the problem.

15. Maggie has a ribbon 27 feet long. What is the length of the ribbon in yards?

    Equation: _____

    Answer: _____

16. Mañuel has 15 goldfish. This is 6 more than Quinn has. How many goldfish does Quinn have?

    Equation: _____

    Answer: _____

17. In their yearbook photo, students in the chorus stood in four rows with 13 students in each row. How many students are in the photo?

    Equation: _____

    Answer: _____

18. Julie bought 19 beads at the craft store. Now she has 36 beads. How many beads did she have before she went to the craft store?

    Equation: _____

    Answer: _____

19. **Stretch Your Thinking** Rashid bought some baseball cards. After giving 7 cards to his friend Grace, he arranged the remaining cards in 6 rows of 4. How many cards did he buy?

    Equation: _____

    Answer: _____

Introducing the MathBoard

Homework

1. Write a chain of equivalent fractions for the shaded parts.

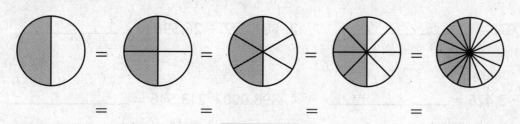

___ = ___ = ___ = ___ = ___

Use the number lines to complete Exercises 2–7.

Fourths

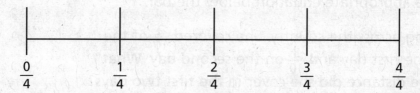

Eighths

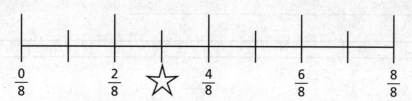

Twelfths

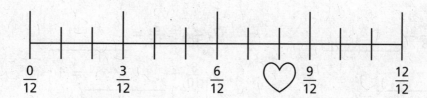

2. What fraction is marked by the star? _____

3. What fraction is marked by the heart? _____

4. If you have $\frac{3}{4}$ cup of flour, how many eighths do you have?

   _____

5. If you have $\frac{3}{12}$ of an orange, how many fourths do you have?

   _____

6. Which is greater, $\frac{3}{4}$ or $\frac{10}{12}$? _____

7. Give two equivalent fractions for $\frac{6}{8}$. _____

Name _____   **Date** _____

Remembering

Add or subtract.

1. $4,560 + 52,973 =$ _____

2. $581,002 + 26,596 =$ _____

3. $4,300,129 + 3,426 =$ _____

4. $398,000 - 213,546 =$ _____

5. Solve the problem below by circling parts of the fraction bar. Write the appropriate equation below the bar.

Molly is driving across the country. She covered $\frac{2}{10}$ of the distance on the first day and $\frac{3}{10}$ on the second day. What fraction of the distance did she cover in the first two days?

_____

Complete.

6. $\frac{1}{8} + \frac{1}{8} + \frac{1}{8} + \frac{1}{8} =$ _____

7. $\frac{7}{10} + \frac{3}{10} =$ _____

8. $\frac{4}{5} - \frac{1}{5} =$ _____

9. $\frac{8}{10} +$ _____ $= 1$

10. _____ $+ \frac{2}{3} = 1$

11. $1 - \frac{3}{4} =$ _____

12. Stretch Your Thinking Alyssa said that $\frac{6}{8}$ and $\frac{9}{12}$ are not equivalent because there is no whole number you can multiply both parts of $\frac{6}{8}$ by to get $\frac{9}{12}$. Is she correct? Explain.

_____

_____

_____

_____

Explain Equivalent Fractions

1. Write a chain of equivalent fractions for the shaded parts.

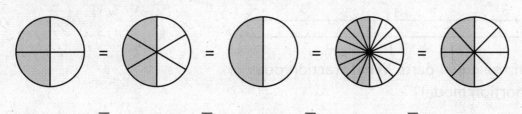

= _____ = _____ = _____ = _____

Write the multiplier or divisor for each pair of equivalent fractions.

2. $\frac{4}{12} = \frac{1}{3}$

Divisor = _____

3. $\frac{2}{9} = \frac{6}{27}$

Multiplier = _____

4. $\frac{6}{60} = \frac{1}{10}$

Divisor = _____

5. $\frac{3}{10} = \frac{15}{50}$

Multiplier = _____

6. $\frac{21}{56} = \frac{3}{8}$

Divisor = _____

7. $\frac{5}{7} = \frac{30}{42}$

Multiplier = _____

8. $\frac{4}{16} = \frac{1}{4}$

Divisor = _____

9. $\frac{5}{9} = \frac{25}{45}$

Multiplier = _____

10. $\frac{10}{60} = \frac{1}{6}$

Divisor = _____

11. $\frac{3}{7} = \frac{18}{42}$

Multiplier = _____

12. $\frac{24}{56} = \frac{3}{7}$

Divisor = _____

13. $\frac{5}{6} = \frac{35}{42}$

Multiplier = _____

Complete each exercise about the pairs of fraction bars.

14. What equivalent fractions are shown? _____

15. Identify the multiplier. _____

16. What equivalent fractions are shown? _____

17. Identify the divisor. _____

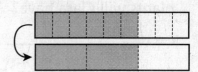

18. Write a chain with at least six equivalent fractions.

_____ = _____ = _____ = _____ = _____

Remembering

In Exercises 1–3, use this fraction bar.

1. Shade two of the equal parts. What fraction does the shaded portion model?

_____

2. Split each equal part (each unit fraction) into two equal parts. What fraction does the shaded portion model now?

_____

3. Fill in the boxes to show how you unsimplified the original fraction.

$$\frac{2 \times \boxed{}}{3 \times \boxed{}} = \frac{\boxed{}}{\boxed{}}$$

Solve.   *Show your work.*

4. A restaurant has 60 plates. One night, 9 groups of 6 people ate dinner at the restaurant at the same time. How many plates were not used by these diners?

_____

5. Clara has a garden that is 7 feet wide and 4 feet long. She has 30 tomato plants to put in the garden. Each plant needs 1 square foot of space. How many leftover plants will Clara have?

_____

6. **Stretch Your Thinking** Carol's bookshelf has 4 shelves with 6 books on each. Her brother Robert has 3 shelves with 7 books on each. They want to combine their books. If they put 9 books on a shelf, how many shelves will they need?

_____

Homework

Compare.

1. $\frac{5}{8}$ ◯ $\frac{5}{9}$ 2. $\frac{1}{5}$ ◯ $\frac{1}{4}$ 3. $\frac{2}{5}$ ◯ $\frac{3}{5}$

4. $\frac{6}{8}$ ◯ $\frac{2}{3}$ 5. $\frac{10}{11}$ ◯ $\frac{11}{12}$ 6. $\frac{3}{8}$ ◯ $\frac{5}{12}$

7. $\frac{5}{12}$ ◯ $\frac{4}{7}$ 8. $\frac{1}{3}$ ◯ $\frac{4}{9}$ 9. $\frac{1}{4}$ ◯ $\frac{2}{9}$

10. $\frac{1}{12}$ ◯ $\frac{1}{15}$ 11. $\frac{7}{10}$ ◯ $\frac{11}{15}$ 12. $\frac{12}{25}$ ◯ $\frac{51}{100}$

Solve.   *Show your work.*

13. During his first season on the school football team, Wade made 5 of the 9 field goals he tried. During his second season, he made 11 of the 15 field goals he tried. In which season did he make the greater fraction of the field goals he tried?

_____

14. Mañuela bought $\frac{11}{12}$ yard of polka dot fabric and $\frac{7}{9}$ yard of flowered fabric. Which fabric did she buy more of?

_____

15. Of the 7 pens in Ms. Young's desk, 3 are blue. Of the 9 pens in Mr. Fox's desk, 5 are blue. Which teacher has a greater fraction of pens that are blue?

_____

16. Mr. Sommers spent 10 minutes of his 50-minute math period reviewing homework. Mr. Young spent 12 minutes of his 60-minute math period reviewing homework. Which teacher spent a greater fraction of his math period reviewing homework?

_____

Remembering

Complete.

1. $\frac{1}{4} + \frac{1}{4} + \frac{1}{4} =$ _____

2. $\frac{8}{9} - \frac{4}{9} =$ _____

3. $\frac{4}{5} + \frac{1}{5} =$ _____

4. $\frac{3}{8} + \frac{3}{8} =$ _____

Write the multiplier or divisor for each pair of equivalent fractions.

5. $\frac{5}{6} = \frac{10}{12}$

Multiplier = _____

6. $\frac{12}{15} = \frac{4}{5}$

Divisor = _____

7. $\frac{3}{4} = \frac{18}{24}$

Multiplier = _____

8. $\frac{25}{50} = \frac{5}{10}$

Divisor = _____

9. $\frac{1}{4} = \frac{7}{28}$

Multiplier = _____

10. $\frac{11}{22} = \frac{1}{2}$

Divisor = _____

Complete the chain of equivalent fractions.

11. $\frac{2}{5} =$ _____ $=$ _____ $=$ _____ $=$ _____ $=$ _____

12. $\frac{5}{9} =$ _____ $=$ _____ $=$ _____ $=$ _____ $=$ _____

Solve.

13. Stretch Your Thinking Harry ate $\frac{4}{8}$ of a large pizza. Aidan ate $\frac{1}{2}$ of a small pizza. Harry said that since $\frac{4}{8}$ is equivalent to $\frac{1}{2}$, he and Aidan ate the same amount of pizza. Is he correct? Explain.

_____

_____

_____

_____

Name the mixed number shown by the shaded parts.

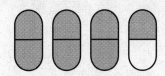 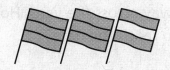

1. _____

2. _____

3. _____

Write the mixed number as a fraction.

4. $2\frac{1}{3}$ = _____

5. $4\frac{2}{5}$ = _____

6. $3\frac{3}{4}$ = _____

7. $1\frac{5}{8}$ = _____

Write the fraction as a mixed number.

8. $\frac{7}{6}$ = _____

9. $\frac{8}{3}$ = _____

10. $\frac{9}{2}$ = _____

11. $\frac{10}{7}$ = _____

Complete. Give the answer as a mixed number.

12. $\frac{3}{5} + \frac{4}{5}$ = _____

13. $\frac{6}{4} + \frac{3}{4}$ = _____

14. $\frac{2}{9} + \frac{8}{9}$ = _____

15. $7 + \frac{2}{3}$ = _____

Solve.

Show your work.

16. Alicia walked $\frac{7}{8}$ mile on Saturday and $\frac{6}{8}$ mile on Sunday. How far did she walk over the weekend? Give the answer as a mixed number.

_____

17. The dark chain is $\frac{5}{12}$ yard long. The light one is $\frac{9}{12}$ yard long. How long will they be if they are joined? Give the answer as a mixed number.

_____

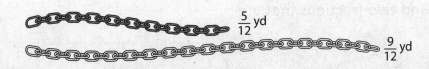

$\frac{5}{12}$ yd

$\frac{9}{12}$ yd

Remembering

Solve.

1. The dog has gone $\frac{5}{8}$ of the way across the yard. How much farther does it have to go to reach the gate?

   _____

2. The cat has gone $\frac{7}{16}$ of the way across the yard. How much farther does it have to go to reach the gate?

   _____

3. I cleaned $\frac{6}{9}$ of my room, and my friend cleaned $\frac{2}{9}$ of my room. How much of my room do we still have to clean?

   _____

4. Mrs. Spencer's class is signing up to play sports. $\frac{8}{26}$ of the students want to play soccer and $\frac{12}{26}$ want to play basketball. The rest of the students want to play baseball. What fraction of the students wants to play baseball?

   _____

Compare.

5. $\frac{2}{6}$ ◯ $\frac{1}{6}$ 6. $\frac{4}{9}$ ◯ $\frac{4}{10}$ 7. $\frac{7}{12}$ ◯ $\frac{13}{24}$

8. $\frac{3}{5}$ ◯ $\frac{1}{3}$ 9. $\frac{4}{6}$ ◯ $\frac{6}{9}$ 10. $\frac{4}{5}$ ◯ $\frac{5}{6}$

11. $\frac{7}{12}$ ◯ $\frac{3}{4}$ 12. $\frac{3}{5}$ ◯ $\frac{4}{9}$ 13. $\frac{7}{9}$ ◯ $\frac{7}{8}$

14. **Stretch Your Thinking** Find two fractions that are between $\frac{3}{5}$ and $\frac{4}{5}$.

   _____

Fractions Greater Than One

Homework

Add or subtract.

1. $\frac{3}{5} + \frac{4}{5}$

2. $\frac{6}{4} + \frac{3}{4}$

3. $4\frac{2}{9} + 2\frac{7}{9}$

4. $1\frac{7}{8} + 3\frac{3}{8}$

5. $1\frac{7}{9} - \frac{4}{9}$

6. $4\frac{6}{7} - 2\frac{5}{7}$

7. $6\frac{4}{5} - 3\frac{2}{5}$

8. $25\frac{5}{8} - 10\frac{1}{8}$

9. $4\frac{1}{2} + 5\frac{1}{2}$

10. $3\frac{1}{7} + 2\frac{1}{7}$

11. $1\frac{5}{7} + 1\frac{3}{7}$

12. $50\frac{1}{3} + 50\frac{1}{3}$

13. $2 - \frac{1}{3}$

14. $5\frac{3}{8} - 2\frac{7}{8}$

15. $2\frac{1}{6} - 1\frac{5}{6}$

Solve.

Show your work.

16. I made a clay snake $9\frac{5}{8}$ inches long, but a section $1\frac{7}{8}$ inches long broke off. How long is the snake now?

_____

17. A group of campers hiked for $5\frac{3}{4}$ hours today and $6\frac{3}{4}$ hours yesterday. How many hours did they hike in all?

_____

18. Deacon had $12\frac{1}{3}$ ounces of juice, but he drank $3\frac{2}{3}$ ounces. How much juice is left?

_____

Remembering

Complete to form equivalent fractions.

1. $\dfrac{1}{2} = \dfrac{4}{\boxed{}}$

2. $\dfrac{12}{\boxed{}} = \dfrac{4}{5}$

3. $\dfrac{6}{7} = \dfrac{\boxed{}}{28}$

4. $\dfrac{4}{\boxed{}} = \dfrac{\boxed{}}{9}$

5. $\dfrac{25}{100} = \dfrac{\boxed{}}{\boxed{}}$

6. $\dfrac{\boxed{}}{8} = \dfrac{3}{\boxed{}}$

Compare.

7. $\dfrac{3}{10} \bigcirc \dfrac{3}{8}$

8. $\dfrac{4}{5} \bigcirc \dfrac{5}{6}$

9. $\dfrac{5}{7} \bigcirc \dfrac{2}{3}$

10. $\dfrac{5}{6} \bigcirc \dfrac{19}{24}$

11. $\dfrac{4}{15} \bigcirc \dfrac{3}{10}$

12. $\dfrac{1}{49} \bigcirc \dfrac{1}{50}$

Solve.

Show your work.

13. Rosá got 5 out of 7 answers correct on her science quiz. Her older sister Ana got 4 answers out of 6 correct on her science quiz. Which sister answered a greater fraction of the questions correctly?

_____

14. The number 85% is equivalent to the fraction $\dfrac{85}{100}$. Pablo spelled 21 out of 25 words correctly on his spelling test. Is this more or less than 85% of the words?

_____

15. **Stretch Your Thinking** Marla ate $\dfrac{3}{8}$ of a small pepperoni pizza and $\dfrac{2}{8}$ of a small cheese pizza. Damien ate $\dfrac{3}{12}$ of a small veggie pizza and $\dfrac{5}{12}$ of a small mushroom pizza. Who ate a greater fraction of a whole pizza?

_____

Homework

Add.

1. $\frac{1}{3} + \frac{1}{2}$

2. $\frac{7}{10} + \frac{1}{5}$

3. $\frac{2}{9} + \frac{1}{6}$

4. $\frac{5}{32} + \frac{1}{4}$

5. $\frac{1}{6} + \frac{2}{3}$

6. $\frac{5}{11} + \frac{1}{2}$

7. $\frac{3}{16} + \frac{3}{4}$

8. $\frac{3}{7} + \frac{1}{3}$

9. $\frac{5}{12} + \frac{3}{8}$

Solve.   *Show your work.*

10. Of the people who attended the school play, $\frac{5}{12}$ were students and $\frac{1}{8}$ were teachers. What fraction of the total audience were students or teachers?

_____

11. Mara bought $\frac{2}{3}$ yard of yellow ribbon and $\frac{1}{4}$ yard of blue ribbon. How many yards of ribbon did she buy altogether?

_____

12. For breakfast, Oliver drank $\frac{5}{16}$ of a pitcher of juice. His brother Joey drank $\frac{3}{8}$ of the pitcher of juice. What fraction of a pitcher did they drink together?

_____

13. A recipe calls for $\frac{1}{3}$ cup of brown sugar and $\frac{3}{4}$ cup of white sugar. How much sugar is this altogether?

_____

Remembering

Solve for *n* or *d*.

1. $\frac{1}{6} = \frac{n}{24}$ _____

2. $\frac{3}{4} = \frac{15}{d}$ _____

3. $\frac{9}{54} = \frac{1}{d}$ _____

4. $\frac{10}{18} = \frac{n}{9}$ _____

5. $\frac{3}{7} = \frac{18}{d}$ _____

6. $\frac{3}{5} = \frac{n}{40}$ _____

7. $\frac{27}{36} = \frac{n}{4}$ _____

8. $\frac{14}{49} = \frac{2}{d}$ _____

9. $\frac{5}{6} = \frac{n}{48}$ _____

10. $\frac{1}{3} = \frac{20}{d}$ _____

11. $\frac{21}{56} = \frac{3}{d}$ _____

12. $\frac{20}{25} = \frac{n}{5}$ _____

Add or subtract.

13. $1\frac{1}{3} + 2\frac{1}{3}$ _____

14. $3\frac{3}{5} - 1\frac{1}{5}$ _____

15. $6\frac{3}{8} + 3\frac{5}{8}$ _____

16. $6\frac{3}{8} - 3\frac{5}{8}$ _____

17. $1\frac{5}{6} + 2\frac{5}{6}$ _____

18. $7 - 5\frac{1}{4}$ _____

Compare.

19. $\frac{3}{4} \bigcirc \frac{6}{7}$

20. $\frac{7}{15} \bigcirc \frac{2}{5}$

21. $\frac{1}{8} \bigcirc \frac{3}{20}$

22. $\frac{6}{100} \bigcirc \frac{6}{101}$

23. $\frac{19}{20} \bigcirc \frac{20}{21}$

24. $\frac{4}{5} \bigcirc \frac{7}{9}$

Solve.

Show your work.

25. In a hockey game, Seth took 12 shots and scored 3 times. Zak took 10 shots and scored twice. Who scored on a greater fraction of his shots?

_____

26. Jia rode her bike $7\frac{7}{8}$ miles in the morning and another $6\frac{5}{8}$ miles in the afternoon. How many miles did she ride altogether?

_____

27. **Stretch Your Thinking** Last season, Jenny made 3 out of every 4 free throws she took. If she took 48 free throws, how many did she make?

_____

Homework

Subtract.

1. $\frac{1}{3} - \frac{1}{7}$

2. $\frac{4}{5} - \frac{8}{15}$

3. $\frac{5}{6} - \frac{2}{9}$

4. $\frac{61}{100} - \frac{7}{25}$

5. $\frac{4}{7} - \frac{1}{6}$

6. $\frac{6}{11} - \frac{1}{2}$

Circle the greater fraction. Then write and solve a subtraction problem to find the difference of the fractions.

7. $\frac{9}{10}$ $\frac{11}{12}$ _____

8. $\frac{5}{18}$ $\frac{1}{3}$ _____

Solve.   *Show your work.*

9. Marly passes the library on her way to school. The distance from Marly's house to the library is $\frac{3}{8}$ mile. The distance from Marly's house to the school is $\frac{4}{5}$ mile. How far is it from the library to Marly's school?

_____

10. Tim spends about $\frac{1}{3}$ of each weekday sleeping and about $\frac{7}{24}$ of each weekday in school.

   a. What fraction of a weekday does Tim spend either sleeping or in school?

   _____

   b. Is this more or less than $\frac{1}{2}$ a day? _____

   c. How much more or less? _____

Name _____ **Date** _____

Remembering

Write each fraction as a mixed number.

1. $\frac{11}{5}$ = _____

2. $\frac{21}{8}$ = _____

3. $\frac{57}{6}$ = _____

Write each mixed number as a fraction.

4. $1\frac{5}{6}$ = _____

5. $11\frac{2}{3}$ = _____

6. $6\frac{1}{9}$ = _____

Add or subtract.

7. $\frac{3}{7} + \frac{2}{7}$

8. $\frac{7}{10} - \frac{3}{10}$

9. $\frac{3}{10} + \frac{2}{5}$

10. $2\frac{1}{6} + 3\frac{5}{6}$

11. $6\frac{11}{12} - 2\frac{5}{12}$

12. $5\frac{1}{3} - 1\frac{2}{3}$

13. $4\frac{3}{4} + 4\frac{3}{4}$

14. $4 - 3\frac{5}{8}$

15. $\frac{3}{11} + \frac{1}{3}$

Solve.

Show your work.

16. Ayala and Sam were partners on a science project. Ayala spent $2\frac{3}{4}$ hours working on the project. Sam spent $1\frac{3}{4}$ hours working on the project. How long did they work altogether?

_____

17. **Stretch Your Thinking** Marti grouped all her CDs into separate categories. She said, "$\frac{2}{5}$ of my CDs are rock music, $\frac{1}{6}$ are jazz, $\frac{1}{3}$ are hip hop, and $\frac{1}{4}$ are country music." Explain why Marti's statement cannot be correct.

_____

_____

_____

Subtract Unlike Fractions

Homework

Add or subtract.

1. $7\frac{1}{2}$
$+\ 6\frac{5}{8}$

2. $2\frac{3}{5}$
$+\ 5\frac{1}{4}$

3. $5\frac{3}{8}$
$+\ 2\frac{3}{4}$

4. $3\frac{4}{15}$
$-\ 1\frac{1}{5}$

5. $9\frac{5}{6}$
$-\ 4\frac{1}{8}$

6. $1\frac{1}{9}$
$+\ 3\frac{5}{8}$

7. $8\frac{1}{6}$
$-\ 2\frac{7}{12}$

8. $6\frac{7}{9}$
$-\ 4\frac{2}{3}$

9. $3\frac{9}{14}$
$-\ 1\frac{2}{7}$

Solve.   *Show your work.*

10. Last year my elm tree was $8\frac{5}{6}$ feet tall. This year it is $10\frac{1}{12}$ feet tall. How much did it grow in one year?

11. Luis rode his bicycle $2\frac{3}{10}$ miles before lunch. He rode $1\frac{1}{4}$ miles after lunch. How far did Luis ride altogether?

12. Carrie spent $2\frac{1}{2}$ hours trimming bushes and $1\frac{1}{4}$ hours weeding the garden. She is supposed to work in the yard for 5 hours. How much longer does she need to work?

Remembering

Add or subtract. Try to do these in your head.

1. $3\frac{1}{4} + 2\frac{3}{4} =$ _____

2. $2\frac{3}{4} - \frac{1}{4} =$ _____

3. $3\frac{2}{5} + 4\frac{4}{5} =$ _____

4. $6\frac{6}{7} - 5\frac{2}{7} =$ _____

5. $8\frac{2}{3} + 1\frac{2}{3} =$ _____

6. $5\frac{6}{7} - 1\frac{2}{7} =$ _____

7. $3\frac{3}{5} + 3\frac{3}{5} =$ _____

8. $7\frac{7}{8} - 3\frac{3}{8} =$ _____

9. $5\frac{3}{8} + 3\frac{5}{8} =$ _____

Write the fractions in order from least to greatest.

10. $\frac{1}{9}, \frac{1}{3}, \frac{1}{6}, \frac{1}{2}$ _____

11. $\frac{4}{9}, \frac{2}{9}, \frac{8}{9}, \frac{1}{9}$ _____

12. $\frac{2}{3}, \frac{3}{5}, \frac{1}{2}, \frac{3}{4}$ _____

13. $\frac{11}{15}, \frac{3}{5}, \frac{2}{3}, \frac{19}{30}$ _____

List three fractions equivalent to the given fraction.

14. $\frac{1}{5}$ _____

15. $\frac{15}{18}$ _____

16. $\frac{4}{7}$ _____

17. $\frac{9}{12}$ _____

Solve.   *Show your work.*

18. Ted is making a bread recipe that uses $3\frac{1}{4}$ cups of flour and a muffin recipe that uses $2\frac{3}{4}$ cups of flour.

   a. How much more flour is in the bread than in the muffins?

   _____

   b. How much flour does Ted need for both recipes?

   _____

19. Stretch Your Thinking Find the values of x and y in the drawing at the right.

   $x =$ _____ inches

   $y =$ _____ inches

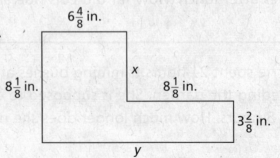

Solve with Unlike Mixed Numbers

Homework

Add or subtract.

1. 3

  $- 1\frac{2}{5}$

2. $2\frac{7}{10}$

  $+ 2\frac{4}{5}$

3. $7\frac{5}{9}$

  $- 3\frac{2}{15}$

4. $4\frac{5}{6}$

  $+ \frac{6}{7}$

5. $5\frac{1}{8}$

  $- 4\frac{1}{5}$

6. $4\frac{79}{100}$

  $+ 5\frac{9}{10}$

7. $\frac{13}{16}$

  $+ \frac{2}{3}$

8. $8\frac{1}{4}$

  $- 3\frac{9}{20}$

9. $7\frac{8}{9}$

  $+ 9\frac{7}{8}$

Solve.

10. The Taylors have four dogs. Molly eats $4\frac{1}{2}$ cups of food each day, Roscoe eats $3\frac{2}{3}$ cups, Milo eats $1\frac{3}{4}$ cups, and Fifi eats $\frac{3}{4}$ cup. How much do the Taylors' dogs eat each day altogether?

_____

11. Refer to Problem 10. How much more food does Molly eat each day than Roscoe?

_____

12. The vet told the Taylors (from Problem 10) to decrease the amount Molly eats by $\frac{3}{4}$ cup. After Molly's food is adjusted, will she eat more or less than Roscoe each day? How much more or less?

_____

Name _____ Date _____

Remembering

What mixed number is shown by each shaded part?

1.

2.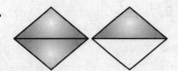

3.

_____ _____ _____

Answer the questions about the bar graph. Give your answers as simple fractions.

4. How many cookies are there altogether? _____

5. What fraction of the cookies are chocolate chip?

_____

6. What fraction of the cookies are oatmeal? _____

7. What fraction of the cookies are peanut butter?

_____

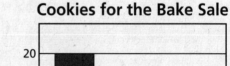

Cookies for the Bake Sale

8. Melanie baked 25 cookies. Did she bake more or less than half of the cookies? _____

How do you know?

_____

_____

9. Stretch Your Thinking Colby nailed together four wood boards as shown at the right. All four boards are $5\frac{1}{2}$ inches wide.

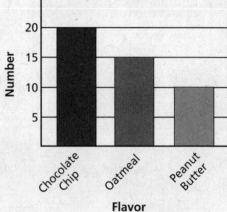

a. Find the perimeter of the outside rectangle.

_____

b. Find the perimeter of the inside rectangle.

_____

Practice with Unlike Mixed Numbers

Homework

Use benchmarks of 0, $\frac{1}{2}$, and 1 to estimate the sum or difference.
Then find the actual sum or difference.

1. $\frac{2}{5} + \frac{4}{7}$

Estimate: _____

Sum: _____

2. $\frac{13}{20} - \frac{3}{10}$

Estimate: _____

Difference: _____

3. $\frac{13}{18} + \frac{1}{2}$

Estimate: _____

Sum: _____

Estimate the sum or difference by rounding each mixed number to
the nearest whole number. Then find the actual sum or difference.

4. $3\frac{5}{8} - 1\frac{1}{2}$

Estimate: _____

Difference: _____

5. $6\frac{4}{9} + 5\frac{7}{12}$

Estimate: _____

Sum: _____

6. $7\frac{11}{18} - 4\frac{1}{15}$

Estimate: _____

Difference: _____

Tell whether the answer is reasonable or unreasonable.
Explain how you decided.

7. $2\frac{1}{5} + 5\frac{1}{3} = 7\frac{8}{15}$

_____

_____

_____

8. $\frac{7}{8} - \frac{2}{11} = \frac{9}{19}$

_____

_____

9. $\frac{3}{8} + \frac{4}{5} = \frac{7}{40}$

_____

_____

10. $4\frac{1}{3} - 1\frac{5}{6} = 2\frac{1}{2}$

_____

_____

Solve.

11. Estimate the difference $8\frac{7}{12} - 4\frac{7}{8} - \frac{4}{10}$.
Explain how you found the answer.

_____

_____

_____

Remembering

Add or subtract. Give your answer in simplest form.

1. $\begin{array}{r} 4 \\ -\ 3\frac{7}{8} \\ \hline \end{array}$

2. $\begin{array}{r} 5\frac{1}{2} \\ +\ 6\frac{3}{4} \\ \hline \end{array}$

3. $\begin{array}{r} 3\frac{1}{10} \\ -\ 1\frac{5}{6} \\ \hline \end{array}$

4. $\begin{array}{r} \frac{6}{7} \\ +\ \frac{3}{5} \\ \hline \end{array}$

5. $\begin{array}{r} 10\frac{3}{8} \\ -\ 1\frac{7}{8} \\ \hline \end{array}$

6. $\begin{array}{r} 2\frac{13}{25} \\ +\ 3\frac{99}{100} \\ \hline \end{array}$

Compare.

7. $\dfrac{5}{7} \bigcirc \dfrac{5}{9}$

8. $\dfrac{99}{100} \bigcirc \dfrac{100}{101}$

9. $\dfrac{7}{15} \bigcirc \dfrac{9}{20}$

10. $\dfrac{6}{11} \bigcirc \dfrac{4}{9}$

11. $\dfrac{1}{21} \bigcirc \dfrac{1}{22}$

12. $\dfrac{5}{16} \bigcirc \dfrac{1}{4}$

Solve.   *Show your work.*

13. On the first math test, Octavia answered 24 out of 30 questions correctly. On the second math test, she answered 19 out of 25 questions correctly. On which test did she answer the greater fraction of the questions correctly?

_____

14. **Stretch Your Thinking** Isidro is riding his bike 22 miles to the art museum. He rode $7\frac{1}{2}$ miles and then took a break. Since his break, he has ridden $5\frac{7}{10}$ mile. How much farther does he have to ride to get to the museum?

_____

Homework

Solve. Explain why your answer is reasonable.

Show your work.

1. Zoe had a board $5\frac{1}{4}$ feet long. She cut off a piece. Now the board is $3\frac{5}{6}$ feet long. How long was the piece she cut off?

   Answer: _____

   Why is the answer reasonable?

   _____

   _____

2. A rectangle has a length of $10\frac{3}{16}$ inches and a width of $6\frac{7}{8}$ inches. What is the perimeter of the rectangle?

   Answer: _____

   Why is the answer reasonable?

   _____

   _____

3. Max is making trail mix. He combines $\frac{2}{5}$ pound of dried fruit and $\frac{1}{3}$ pound of mixed nuts. He adds sunflower seeds to make a total of 1 pound. What is the weight of the seeds?

   Answer: _____

   Why is the answer reasonable?

   _____

   _____

4. At the start of party, a bowl contains 16 pints of punch. Guests drink $10\frac{1}{4}$ pints. Then the host adds another $7\frac{1}{2}$ pints to the bowl. How much punch is in the bowl now?

   Answer: _____

   Why is the answer reasonable?

   _____

   _____

Remembering

Tell whether the answer is reasonable or unreasonable. Explain how you decided.

1. $\dfrac{8}{9} + \dfrac{1}{10} = \dfrac{39}{90}$

_____

_____

2. $5\dfrac{1}{6} - 4\dfrac{2}{7} = 2\dfrac{37}{42}$

_____

_____

3. $\dfrac{11}{12} - \dfrac{7}{8} = \dfrac{1}{24}$

_____

_____

4. $5\dfrac{5}{6} + 1\dfrac{3}{4} = 5\dfrac{1}{12}$

_____

_____

Add or subtract.

5. $\dfrac{7}{8} + \dfrac{5}{8} =$ _____

6. $\dfrac{4}{7} + \dfrac{2}{3} =$ _____

7. $\dfrac{7}{15} - \dfrac{3}{10} =$ _____

8. $\dfrac{3}{4} - \dfrac{5}{12} =$ _____

9. $5\dfrac{4}{5} - 2\dfrac{1}{3} =$ _____

10. $7\dfrac{5}{6} + 2\dfrac{11}{12} =$ _____

Compare.

11. $\dfrac{5}{8} \bigcirc \dfrac{5}{9}$

12. $1\dfrac{7}{12} \bigcirc 1\dfrac{2}{3}$

13. $\dfrac{5}{9} \bigcirc \dfrac{3}{7}$

14. $\dfrac{1}{89} \bigcirc \dfrac{1}{90}$

15. $\dfrac{5}{18} \bigcirc \dfrac{2}{9}$

16. $\dfrac{65}{66} \bigcirc \dfrac{55}{56}$

Solve.

17. **Stretch Your Thinking** Find two mixed numbers such that when you estimate their sum by rounding to the nearest whole number you get a *different* estimate than when you round to the nearest half. Demonstrate that your numbers satisfy this condition.

_____

_____

_____

_____

Real World Problems

Homework

In the space below, design and sketch a bird hotel.
Assume your design will be made from wood,
and includes these characteristics.

▸ Walls not exposed to weathering are $\frac{1}{4}$-inch
thick.

▸ Walls exposed to weathering are $\frac{1}{2}$-inch thick.

▸ The rooms are identical.

State the number of birds your design will
accommodate, and the dimensions of one room.
Then use the dimensions to compute the overall
length, width, and height of your hotel.

Remembering

Add or subtract. Give your answer in simplest form.

1. $7\frac{1}{4}$
$-4\frac{5}{6}$

2. $1\frac{9}{10}$
$+1\frac{9}{10}$

3. 4
$-1\frac{6}{7}$

4. $\frac{7}{10}$
$+1\frac{11}{12}$

5. $4\frac{4}{5}$
$-1\frac{7}{8}$

6. $3\frac{5}{12}$
$+1\frac{2}{3}$

Compare.

7. $\frac{1}{57} \bigcirc \frac{1}{47}$

8. $\frac{5}{7} \bigcirc \frac{4}{5}$

9. $\frac{14}{15} \bigcirc \frac{15}{16}$

10. $\frac{5}{6} \bigcirc \frac{2}{3}$

11. $15\frac{3}{8} \bigcirc 15\frac{7}{10}$

12. $14\frac{1}{10} \bigcirc 13\frac{9}{10}$

Solve.   *Show your work.*

13. Blake watched $\frac{1}{6}$ of a movie on Friday, $\frac{3}{5}$ of the movie on Saturday, and the rest on Sunday. What fraction of the movie did he watch on Sunday?

_____

14. **Stretch Your Thinking** Marshall surveyed his classmates and found that $\frac{5}{7}$ have a sister, $\frac{1}{2}$ have a brother, and $\frac{3}{14}$ don't have any siblings.

   a. What is the sum of the three fractions?

   _____

   b. Why does it make sense for the sum to be greater than 1 whole?

   _____

   _____

Homework

The following shows how place value and money are related.

| **ones** (dollars) | **tenths** (dimes) | **hundredths** (pennies) | **thousandths** (tenths of a penny) |

Write each fraction as a decimal and then say it.

1. $\frac{349}{1,000}$ _____

2. $\frac{6}{10}$ _____

3. $\frac{58}{100}$ _____

4. $\frac{27}{1,000}$ _____

5. $\frac{2}{10}$ _____

6. $\frac{9}{100}$ _____

7. $\frac{6}{1,000}$ _____

8. $\frac{71}{100}$ _____

9. $\frac{90}{100}$ _____

10. $\frac{843}{1,000}$ _____

11. $\frac{5}{10}$ _____

12. $\frac{4}{100}$ _____

13. $\frac{1}{1,000}$ _____

14. $\frac{45}{100}$ _____

15. $\frac{896}{1,000}$ _____

16. $\frac{58}{1,000}$ _____

Solve.

17. A large building has 1,000 windows, and 5 of the windows need to be replaced. What decimal represents the number of windows that need to be replaced?

_____

18. At a reception, 23 of 100 pieces of wedding cake have been eaten. What decimal number represents the number of pieces of cake that have been eaten?

_____

19. Jody made 10 party invitations. Yesterday she mailed 4 of them. What decimal represents the number of invitations that have been mailed?

_____

20. There are 1,000 vehicles in a stadium parking lot; 422 of the vehicles are trucks. What decimal represents the number of vehicles that are trucks?

_____

21. Mr. Chan handed out eight tenths of his flyers. Write a fraction and a decimal that represents the amount of the flyers that he handed out.

_____

22. Jason has an album that holds 100 trading cards. He has 52 trading cards in the album. Write a fraction and a decimal that represent the amount of the album that is filled.

_____

Remembering

Add.

1. $\frac{1}{3} + \frac{1}{7}$

2. $\frac{1}{5} + \frac{8}{15}$

3. $\frac{3}{8} + \frac{1}{4}$

Subtract.

4. $\frac{4}{5} - \frac{1}{8}$

5. $\frac{5}{6} - \frac{5}{9}$

6. $\frac{3}{5} - \frac{1}{12}$

Add or Subtract.

7. $\begin{array}{r} 5 \\ -\ 3\frac{5}{8} \\ \hline \end{array}$

8. $\begin{array}{r} 8\frac{1}{5} \\ +\ 5\frac{4}{7} \\ \hline \end{array}$

9. $\begin{array}{r} 11\frac{2}{5} \\ -\ 6\frac{3}{20} \\ \hline \end{array}$

Solve.

Show your work.

10. Kennedy served $15\frac{3}{4}$ hours of volunteer service last month. She served $21\frac{5}{6}$ hours of volunteer service this month. How many more hours did she serve this month?

_____

11. **Stretch Your Thinking** Draw a diagram that shows 0.5 and $\frac{1}{2}$ are equivalent.

Decimals as Equal Divisions

Homework

Write a decimal number for each word name.

1. nine thousand, six hundred five and nine tenths

   _____

2. two hundred ten thousand, fifty and nineteen hundredths

   _____

3. three tenths

   _____

4. seven thousandths

   _____

5. eight hundredths

   _____

Write each amount as a decimal number.

6. $\frac{602}{1,000}$ _____   7. $\frac{21}{100}$ _____   8. $4\frac{9}{10}$ _____   9. $14\frac{27}{100}$ _____

10. $35\frac{712}{1,000}$ _____   11. $9\frac{5}{100}$ _____   12. $24\frac{13}{1,000}$ _____   13. $3\frac{68}{100}$ _____

14. $2\frac{1}{1,000}$ _____   15. $63\frac{7}{10}$ _____   16. $\frac{84}{1,000}$ _____   17. $29\frac{4}{1,000}$ _____

18. $8\frac{17}{1,000}$ _____   19. $\frac{6}{100}$ _____   20. $5\frac{106}{1,000}$ _____   21. $37\frac{3}{100}$ _____

Circle the value that is not equivalent to the other values.

22. 2.6   2.60   2.06   2.600   23. 4.07   4.070   4.70   4.0700

24. 65.800   65.8   65.08   65.80   25. 37.6   37.060   37.0600   37.06

26. Write three decimals that are equivalent.

   _____

27. Write the decimals in Exercise 26 as fractions.

   _____

Remembering

Add or Subtract.

1. $8\frac{1}{6}$
    $-3\frac{3}{8}$

2. $6\frac{3}{4}$
    $+2\frac{4}{5}$

3. $9\frac{2}{3}$
    $+5\frac{7}{10}$

Solve.   *Show your work.*

4. Tanner earns 5 credits while playing on a math review
   website. He uses $2\frac{4}{15}$ credits while reviewing fractions.
   How many credits does he have left?

   _____

**Estimate the sum or difference by rounding each mixed
number to the nearest whole number. Then find the actual
sum or difference.**

5. $15\frac{5}{6}$
    $-2\frac{1}{5}$

6. $8\frac{3}{5}$
    $+3\frac{1}{2}$

Estimate: _____   Estimate: _____

Difference: _____   Sum: _____

Write each fraction as a decimal and then say it.

7. $\frac{44}{100}$ _____   8. $\frac{13}{1,000}$ _____   9. $\frac{3}{10}$ _____   10. $\frac{541}{1,000}$ _____

11. **Stretch Your Thinking** Draw two number lines that show
    0.20 and $\frac{1}{5}$ are equivalent.

Write each amount as a decimal number.

1. 9 tenths _____

2. 52 thousandths _____

3. 8 hundredths _____

4. 3 cents _____

5. $\frac{65}{100}$ _____

6. $\frac{548}{1,000}$ _____

7. $\frac{12}{1,000}$ _____

8. $\frac{7}{100}$ _____

9. 4 thousandths _____

Circle the value that is *not* equivalent to the other values.

10. 0.47   0.470   0.407   0.4700

11. 0.5   0.50 $\frac{5}{10}$ 0.05

12. 0.801   0.810   0.81   0.8100

13. 0.700   0.70   0.07   0.7

14. 0.39   0.390 $\frac{39}{100}$ $\frac{39}{1,000}$

15. 0.04   0.40   0.040   0.0400

Compare. Write > (greater than) or < (less than).

16. 0.36 ◯ 0.8

17. 0.405 ◯ 0.62

18. 0.91 ◯ 0.95

19. 0.45 ◯ 0.4

20. 0.836 ◯ 0.83

21. 0.299 ◯ 0.3

22. 0.621 ◯ 0.612

23. 0.7 ◯ 0.07

24. 0.504 ◯ 0.54

A store had the same amount of five fabrics. The chart shows the how much of each fabric is left. Use the data to answer each question.

25. The store sold the most of which fabric? Explain.

_____

26. The store sold the least of which fabric? Explain.

_____

27. The same amount of which fabrics is left? Explain.

_____

Red fabric	0.510 yd
Blue fabric	0.492 yd
Yellow fabric	0.6 yd
White fabric	0.51 yd
Black fabric	0.48 yd

Remembering

Estimate the sum or difference by rounding each mixed number to the nearest whole number. Then find the actual sum or difference.

1. $3\frac{7}{8} + 4\frac{2}{3}$

Estimate: _____

Sum: _____

2. $7\frac{5}{8} - 1\frac{1}{2}$

Estimate: _____

Difference: _____

Solve. Explain how you know your answer is reasonable.

Show your work.

3. Eli practices for a piano recital $3\frac{3}{4}$ hours in one week. In the same week, he practices basketball $1\frac{2}{3}$ hours. How much longer does he practice for his piano recital?

Answer: _____

Why is the answer reasonable?

_____

_____

Write a decimal number for each word name.

4. six hundred two and six tenths

_____

5. five thousandths

_____

6. Stretch Your Thinking Draw two number lines that show 0.200 and $\frac{1}{5}$ are equivalent.

Equate and Compare Thousandths

2-4

Homework

The chart at the right shows the time each
member of a relay team ran during a race.
Use the data to answer each question.

Jack	47.51 sec
Dusty	47.49 sec
Brandon	47.6 sec
Raj	47.57 sec

1. How much longer did Jack run than Dusty?

_____

2. How much time did it take Brandon and Raj to
complete their two legs of the race combined?

_____

3. Which two runners had the greatest difference
in their running times? What is the difference?

_____

Copy each exercise. Then add or subtract.

4. $0.9 + 0.06 =$ _____

5. $0.47 + 0.25 =$ _____

6. $0.56 + 0.91 =$ _____

7. $1.4 - 0.9 =$ _____

8. $5 - 1.5 =$ _____

9. $3.7 - 2.49 =$ _____

10. $0.08 + 0.6 =$ _____

11. $0.48 + 0.39 =$ _____

12. $19 + 1.04 =$ _____

13. $3 - 0.05 =$ _____

14. $4.09 - 0.2 =$ _____

15. $6.07 - 4 =$ _____

Remembering

Use benchmarks of 0, $\frac{1}{2}$, and 1 to estimate the sum or difference. Then find the actual sum or difference.

1. $\frac{7}{12} + \frac{5}{6}$

   Estimate: _____

   Sum: _____

2. $\frac{4}{9} - \frac{7}{18}$

   Estimate: _____

   Difference: _____

Solve. Explain how you know your answer is reasonable.

Show your work.

3. Jordan is making a beaded necklace. Two thirds of the beads she uses are red and $\frac{4}{21}$ of the beads are blue. She wants the rest to be white. What fraction of the beads should be white?

   Answer: _____

   Why is the answer reasonable?

   _____

   _____

   _____

Compare. Write $>$ (greater than) or $<$ (less than).

4. 0.2 $\bigcirc$ 0.19

5. 0.564 $\bigcirc$ 0.602

6. 0.08 $\bigcirc$ 0.8

7. **Stretch Your Thinking** Draw a diagram that shows $0.27 + 0.23 = \frac{1}{2}$.

Adding and Subtracting Decimals

Homework

Use the number 724,062.58 for each exercise.

1. Increase the number by 0.07. _____

2. Decrease the number by 100,000. _____

3. Add 8 in the hundreds place. _____

4. Subtract 2 from the hundredths place. _____

Copy each exercise. Then add or subtract.

5. $37 + 45¢ = _____   **6.** $82.06 + 25¢ = _____   **7.** 59¢ + $4.23 = _____

8. 9 m + 0.05 m = _____   **9.** 92.24 + 3.6 = _____   **10.** 5 m + 0.08 m = _____

11. 231 + 0.26 = _____   **12.** 46.08 + 0.97 = _____   **13.** 6.4 m + 0.07 m = _____

Solve.   *Show your work.*

14. Lina is making curtains and a decorative pillow for her bedroom. She needs 0.75 meter of cloth for the pillow and 4.67 meters for the curtains. How much cloth does she need in all?

_____

15. Olivia is buying a jacket that costs $85.99. The sales tax that will be added to the cost of the jacket is $5.16. What is the total cost of the jacket including sales tax?

_____

Name _____ **Date** _____

Remembering

Compare. Write > (greater than) or < (less than).

1. $\frac{3}{7}$ ◯ $\frac{3}{8}$

2. $\frac{1}{8}$ ◯ $\frac{1}{6}$

3. $\frac{9}{11}$ ◯ $\frac{7}{11}$

4. $\frac{4}{8}$ ◯ $\frac{5}{6}$

5. $\frac{5}{6}$ ◯ $\frac{3}{4}$

6. $\frac{7}{12}$ ◯ $\frac{6}{7}$

Compare. Write > (greater than) or < (less than).

7. 0.17 ◯ 0.28

8. 0.275 ◯ 0.109

9. 0.29 ◯ 0.3

10. 0.61 ◯ 0.58

11. 0.81 ◯ 0.79

12. 0.05 ◯ 0.5

Add or subtract.

13.
```
   0.8
+ 0.07
```

14.
```
   0.22
+ 0.49
```

15.
```
   2.6
 - 0.7
```

16.
```
   5.6
 - 4.87
```

17.
```
   7
 - 3.8
```

18.
```
   0.96
 + 0.17
```

19. **Stretch Your Thinking** Write 4 different mixed decimals that equal 11 wholes. Draw a picture that shows you are correct.

_____

Add Whole Numbers and Decimals

Homework

Copy each exercise. Then subtract.

1. $6,000 - 348 =$ _____   **2.** $7,364 - 937 =$ _____   **3.** $50,821 - 3,617 =$ _____

4. $720.95 - 286.4 =$ _____   **5.** $18,652 - 4.31 =$ _____   **6.** $350.6 - 176.54 =$ _____

Solve.

Show your work.

7. Ahmad had a piece of rope that was 7.14 meters long. He cut off 0.09 meter to practice making knots. What was the length of the rope after the cut?

_____

8. Natasha has a large collection of books. The thickest book measures 4.9 centimeters. The thinnest book measures 1.8 centimeters. What is the difference in thicknesses of those two books?

_____

9. Yoshi saved $1,238.46 for a vacation in Mexico. While in Mexico, she spent $975. What amount of money did Yoshi not spend?

_____

10. Tarantulas are one of the largest spiders on Earth. A tarantula can grow to be about 6.8 centimeters long. A spitting spider can grow to be about 0.9 centimeters long. About how much longer are the largest tarantulas than the largest spitting spiders?

_____

Remembering

Name _____ Date _____

Write the mixed number as a fraction.

1. $1\frac{3}{5} =$ _____

2. $3\frac{1}{8} =$ _____

3. $2\frac{2}{3} =$ _____

4. $4\frac{4}{7} =$ _____

5. $1\frac{1}{3} =$ _____

6. $3\frac{5}{6} =$ _____

Add or subtract.

7. $\begin{array}{r} 6 \\ -\ 4.1 \\ \hline \end{array}$

8. $\begin{array}{r} 0.32 \\ +\ 0.92 \\ \hline \end{array}$

9. $\begin{array}{r} 4.5 \\ -\ 3.77 \\ \hline \end{array}$

10. $44¢ + \$4.87 =$ _____

11. $32¢ + 66¢ =$ _____

12. $0.43\ m + 0.77\ m =$ _____

Solve.

Show your work.

13. When Erin got her puppy, Cuddles, he weighed 788.52 grams. He now weighs 2,313.6 grams more than he did when Erin first brought him home. How much does Cuddles weigh now?

_____

14. **Stretch Your Thinking** Write a subtraction equation with a difference of 54.57. Then draw a number line to show between which two whole numbers the difference lies.

_____

Subtract Whole and Decimal Numbers

Homework

Use what you know about the Commutative Property to solve for *n*.

1. $26,184 + 1,546 = 1,546 + n$

$n =$ _____

2. $17.39 + 12.58 = 12.58 + n$

$n =$ _____

Regroup the numbers using the Associative Property. Then add.

3. $(\frac{7}{10} + \frac{3}{4}) + \frac{1}{4} =$

_____

4. $1.02 + (0.98 + 4.87) =$

_____

5. $2\frac{5}{8} + (\frac{3}{8} + \frac{2}{3}) =$

_____

Use the Distributive Property to rewrite the problem so it has only two factors. Then solve.

6. $(25 \times 9) + (75 \times 9) =$

_____

Group the numbers to make the addition easier. Then add.

7.	8.	9.	10.
20,000	10.75	1.600	$1\frac{7}{11}$
70,000	10.4	1.200	$5\frac{5}{6}$
30,000	10.25	1.200	$\frac{3}{11}$
68,000	10.57	+ 1.479	$2\frac{1}{6}$
+ 80,000	+ 10.6		$+ \frac{1}{11}$

11. On Monday, Mr. Borden ran 4.6 miles in the morning and 0.78 miles that afternoon. On Tuesday, he ran 3.4 miles. How much did he run on Monday and Tuesday all together. Write an equation and solve.

_____

Remembering

Solve.   *Show your work.*

1. Trent is making a week's worth of after-school snacks for himself and his sister. He uses $1\frac{1}{5}$ cups of mixed nuts and $2\frac{3}{4}$ cups of granola. How many cups did he use in all?

   _____

2. Shannon walked $4\frac{7}{8}$ miles and ran $3\frac{1}{2}$ miles during the week. How much further did she walk than run?

   _____

Add.

3. $\$54.25 + 55\cent =$ _____   4. $68\cent + 21\cent =$ _____   5. $92\cent + \$2.39 =$ _____

6. $\quad 0.06$ m
   $+\ 0.9$ m
   _____

7. $\quad 0.44$ m
   $+\ 0.15$ m
   _____

8. $\quad 5.6$ m
   $+\ 0.7$ m
   _____

Subtract.

9. $\quad 70,763$
   $-\quad 2,176$
   _____

10. $\quad 6,982$
   $-\quad\ \ 455$
   _____

11. $\quad 5,000$
   $-\quad\ \ 452$
   _____

12. $\quad 46,872$
   $-\quad\ \ \ 8.28$
   _____

13. $\quad 561.5$
   $-\ 478.49$
   _____

14. $\quad 676.54$
   $-\ 196.9$
   _____

15. **Stretch Your Thinking** Use decimals and fractions in the same equation showing the Commutative Property. Repeat for the Associative Property.

   _____

   _____

Properties and Strategies

Homework

Round to the nearest whole number.

1. 8.36 _____ **2.** 18.7 _____ **3.** 9.831 _____

Round to the nearest tenth.

4. 24.316 _____ **5.** 5.28 _____ **6.** 23.017 _____

Round to the nearest hundredth.

7. 58.635 _____ **8.** 7.214 _____ **9.** 210.097 _____

Estimate each sum or difference.

10. $46.78 − $18.55 _____ **11.** 12.3 + 4.7 _____ **12.** 9.586 + 3.097 _____

Solve. *Show your work.*

13. A decimal number changed to 23.7 after it was rounded. Give a decimal number that is less than 23.7 and another that is greater than 23.7 that each round to 23.7. Explain to what place each number was rounded.

_____

_____

14. When Marla rounded 19.95 to the nearest tenth, she found the number changed to 20. Is this correct? Explain.

_____

15. Peter decided that the total cost for a $24.55 pair of jeans and a $12.25 shirt was $26.80. Was Peter's answer reasonable? Explain why or why not.

_____

16. Biruk wants to buy a book for $15.25 and a book for $4.85. He wants to pay with one $20 bill. Use estimation to decide if this is reasonable. Explain to what place value to round for an estimate that is useful in this situation.

_____

Name _____ **Date** _____

Remembering

Solve.   *Show your work.*

1. Matt pours $3\frac{2}{3}$ cups of orange juice into
   a measuring cup from a large container.
   Then he pours $1\frac{1}{4}$ cups back into the
   container. How much orange juice remains
   in the measuring cup?

   _____

2. The school cafeteria manager orders
   $7\frac{3}{8}$ pounds of red onions and $10\frac{1}{2}$ pounds
   of yellow onions. How many pounds of
   onions did the manager order in all?

   _____

Subtract.

3.	21,445	4.	980.3	5.	774.12
	− 3,548		− 525.35		−248.8

**Use the Distributive Property to rewrite each problem so it
has only two factors. Then solve.**

6. $(5 \times 600) + (5 \times 400) =$ _____

7. $(15 \times 6) + (85 \times 6) =$ _____

8. **Stretch Your Thinking** Name three decimals between 16.4 and 16.5.
   Draw a number line estimating the placement of all five decimals.

   _____

Round and Estimate with Decimals

Homework

Jamal made a bar graph to compare the weights of 4 puppies in the animal shelter.

1. How much did the poodle weigh?

   _____

2. List the puppies in order from heaviest to lightest.

   _____

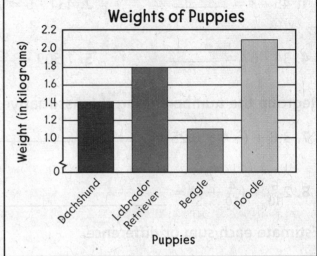

Weights of Puppies

3. What is the combined weights of the Labrador retriever and the beagle?

   _____

4. How much more did the Labrador retriever weigh than the dachshund?

   _____

The table shows the amount of rainfall this month in 4 different cities.

City	Rainfall Amounts
Chester	0.20 cm
Creekside	0.10 cm
Merton	0.05 cm
Warner	0.25 cm

5. Make a bar graph showing this information. Remember to give your graph a title, labels, and a scale.

Chester	Creekside	Merton	Warner

Name _____ **Date** _____

Remembering

Multiply.

1. 45 · 3 = _____

2. 431 · 6 = _____

3. 17 · 32 = _____

4. 34 · 67 = _____

5. 1,509 · 3 = _____

6. 5,098 · 7 = _____

Regroup the numbers using the Associative Property. Then add.

7. 3.6 + (0.4 + 0.25) = _____

8. $2\frac{6}{10} + (\frac{4}{10} + \frac{4}{5})$ = _____

Estimate each sum or difference.

9. 7.535 + 2.706

10. $27.89 − $12.64

11. 11.1 + 9.9

12. Stretch Your Thinking The bar graph shows the heights of bean plants for four students in Mrs. Jarnigan's fourth-grade science class.

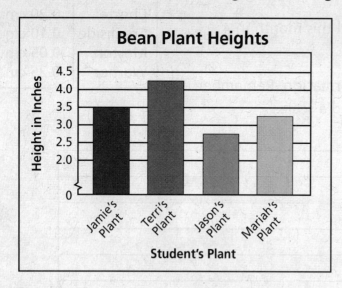

Write a two-step problem using the data from the graph.

_____

_____

_____

_____

Graph with Decimal Numbers

Look again at the table on Student Book page 54. It shows how far from the sun the planets in our solar system orbit. For example, it shows that Jupiter (5.2 AU) orbits *about* 5 times farther from the sun than Earth (1 AU) because $1 \times 5 = 5$.

On a grid where 1 grid square = 1 AU, a dot for Earth would be 1 grid square away from the sun, and a dot for Jupiter would be about 5 grid squares away.

On the left side of the grid below, draw a dot to represent the sun. Then using the scale 1 grid square = 1 AU, draw and label a dot for each of the eight planets to show their relative distances from the sun.

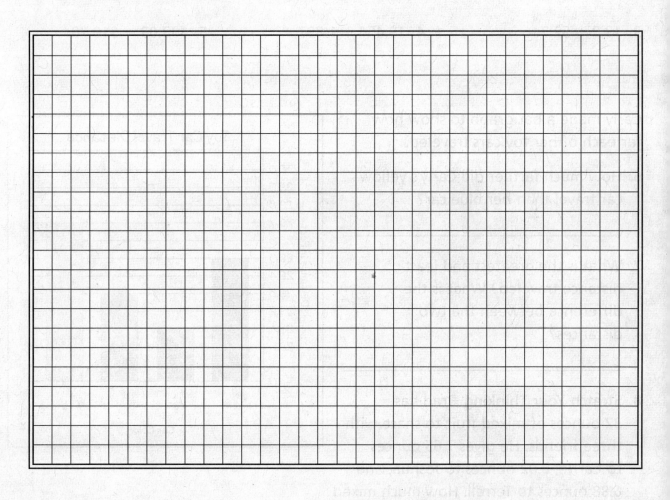

Remembering

Solve.

Show your work.

1. During a movie, Kelley eats $12\frac{2}{7}$ ounces of snack mix and Madison eats $15\frac{3}{4}$ ounces of snack mix. How much did they eat altogether?

_____

2. Caleb practices the piano for $15\frac{2}{3}$ minutes on Monday and $21\frac{1}{2}$ minutes on Tuesday. How much longer did he practice on Tuesday?

_____

Estimate each sum or difference.

3. $13.2 + 52.7$

4. $19.454 + 1.897$

5. $\$33.03 - \$10.78$

Carly made a bar graph to show how far each of her toy cars traveled.

6. How much farther did Carly's yellow car travel than her blue car?

_____

7. What is the greatest and least distance traveled? What is the difference between the two distances?

_____

8. **Stretch Your Thinking** Brad has 32 ounces of mixed fruit to share with three friends. He gives 7.65 ounces to Carrie, 8.02 ounces to Joshua, and 6.88 ounces to Terrell. How much mixed fruit is left for Brad?

_____

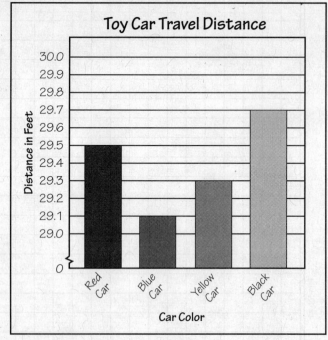

Solve. Write a multiplication equation for each problem.

Miguel swam 6 lengths of the pool. Po Lan swam 3 times as far as Miguel. Lionel swam $\frac{1}{3}$ as far as Miguel.

1. How many lengths did Po Lan swim? _____

   Write the equation. _____

2. How many lengths did Lionel swim? _____

   Write the equation. _____

Chris cut a length of rope that was 12 feet long. Dayna cut a rope 4 times as long as Chris's rope. Benita cut a rope $\frac{1}{4}$ as long as Chris's rope.

3. How long is Dayna's rope? _____

   Write the equation. _____

4. How long is Benita's rope? _____

   Write the equation. _____

Write two statements for each pair of treats. Use the word *times*.

5. Compare cookies and drinks.

   _____

   _____

6. Compare drinks and pizzas.

   _____

   _____

7. Compare cookies and pizzas.

   _____

   _____

Treat	Number
	24
	8
	2

Solve.

8. $\frac{1}{3} \cdot 18 =$ _____   9. $\frac{1}{4}$ of $12 =$ _____   10. $\frac{1}{8} \cdot 32 =$ _____

11. $\frac{1}{9}$ of $27 =$ _____   12. $\frac{1}{8} \cdot 56 =$ _____   13. $\frac{1}{3}$ of $15 =$ _____

Remembering

Use the number lines to complete Exercises 1–3.

Thirds
$$\frac{0}{3} \quad \frac{1}{3} \quad \frac{2}{3} \quad \frac{3}{3}$$

Sixths
$$\frac{0}{6} \quad \frac{1}{6} \quad \frac{2}{6} \quad \frac{3}{6} \quad \frac{4}{6} \quad \frac{5}{6} \quad \frac{6}{6}$$

Twelfths
$$\frac{0}{12} \quad \frac{1}{12} \quad \frac{2}{12} \quad \frac{3}{12} \quad \frac{4}{12} \quad \frac{5}{12} \quad \frac{6}{12} \quad \frac{7}{12} \quad \frac{8}{12} \quad \frac{9}{12} \quad \frac{10}{12} \quad \frac{11}{12} \quad \frac{12}{12}$$

1. If you run $\frac{2}{3}$ mile, how many sixths have you run?

_____

2. If you measure $\frac{5}{6}$ meter, how many twelfths have you measured?

_____

3. If you have $\frac{8}{12}$ of a pizza, how many thirds do you have?

_____

Write each fraction as a decimal.

4. $\frac{76}{1,000} =$ _____

5. $\frac{7}{10} =$ _____

6. $\frac{49}{100} =$ _____

7. $\frac{32}{1,000} =$ _____

Add or subtract.

8. $0.28 + 0.43 =$ _____

9. $0.7 + 0.04 =$ _____

10. $7.8 - 1.95 =$ _____

11. Stretch Your Thinking Draw a diagram that shows $\frac{1}{5}$ times 30 equals 6.

Basic Multiplication Concepts

Homework

Multiply.

1. $\frac{2}{3} \cdot 15 =$ _____

2. $\frac{3}{4} \cdot 8 =$ _____

3. $\frac{7}{8} \cdot 32 =$ _____

4. $\frac{2}{9} \cdot 27 =$ _____

5. $\frac{3}{8} \cdot 56 =$ _____

6. $\frac{3}{4} \cdot 16 =$ _____

7. $\frac{2}{3} \cdot 21 =$ _____

8. $\frac{4}{5} \cdot 35 =$ _____

9. $\frac{5}{7} \cdot 28 =$ _____

10. $\frac{4}{9} \cdot 45 =$ _____

11. $\frac{5}{12} \cdot 24 =$ _____

12. $\frac{9}{10} \cdot 70 =$ _____

13. $\frac{7}{9} \cdot 18 =$ _____

14. $\frac{5}{8} \cdot 80 =$ _____

15. $\frac{4}{15} \cdot 45 =$ _____

Solve.   *Show your work.*

16. Rebecca has 21 math problems to solve. She has solved $\frac{2}{7}$ of them. How many problems has she solved?

   _____

17. Tessa shot 36 free throws. She made 27 of them. What fraction of her free throws did Tessa make?

   _____

18. A carousel has 56 horses. $\frac{3}{8}$ of them are white. How many horses are not white?

   _____

19. Nathan works at a hardware store. Today he sold 48 tools. $\frac{5}{6}$ of the tools he sold were hammers. How many hammers did Nathan sell today?

   _____

Remembering

Complete each exercise about the pairs of fraction bars.

1. What equivalent fractions are shown? _____

2. Identify the multiplier. _____

3. What equivalent fractions are shown? _____

4. Identify the divisor. _____

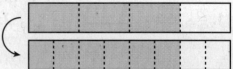

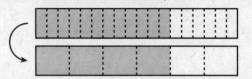

Write each amount as a decimal number.

5. $\frac{84}{1,000}$ _____

6. $\frac{31564}{1,000}$ _____

7. $\frac{1176}{100}$ _____

8. $\frac{876}{1,000}$ _____

Solve. Write a multiplication equation for each problem.

Jonas has 8 sponsors for the school walk-a-thon.
Maura has 3 times as many sponsors as Jonas.
Trenton has $\frac{1}{4}$ as many sponsors as Jonas.

9. How many sponsors does Maura have? _____

Write the equation. _____

10. How many sponsors does Trenton have? _____

Write the equation. _____

11. **Stretch Your Thinking** Hannah and Jo are driving
    separately to a restaurant that is 60 miles away
    from their town. Hannah drives $\frac{3}{5}$ of the distance
    and Jo drives $\frac{5}{6}$ of the distance before stopping for
    gasoline. Who has driven farther? How many
    more miles does each driver need to drive to
    reach the restaurant?

    _____

    _____

    _____

Multiplication with Non-Unit Fractions

The campers in each cabin at Bear Claw Camp held a contest to see who could walk the farthest in one day. Use the sign to answer the questions. Write your answers as fractions.

Otter Ridge 13 mi.
Silver Stream 8 mi.
Fossil Cave 9 mi.
Mammoth Mountain 25 mi.

1. The campers in Cabin A walked $\frac{1}{4}$ of the way to Otter Ridge. How many miles did they walk?

_____

2. The campers in Cabin B walked $\frac{2}{3}$ of the way to Silver Stream. How many miles did they walk?

_____

3. The campers in Cabin C walked $\frac{3}{5}$ of the way to Fossil Cave. How many miles did they walk?

_____

4. The campers in Cabin D walked $\frac{1}{6}$ of the way to Mammoth Mountain. How many miles did they walk?

_____

5. Which group of campers walked the farthest that day?

_____

6. Show $\frac{2}{3}$ of 4 on the number line.

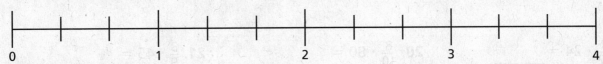

0   1   2   3   4

7. Write $\frac{2}{3}$ of 4 as a fraction. _____

8. Write $\frac{2}{3}$ of 4 as a mixed number. _____

Multiply. Write your answers as fractions.

9. $\frac{2}{7} \cdot 4 =$ _____ **10.** $\frac{2}{3} \cdot 8 =$ _____ **11.** $\frac{5}{6} \cdot 4 =$ _____

12. $\frac{2}{9} \cdot 20 =$ _____ **13.** $\frac{7}{9} \cdot 2 =$ _____ **14.** $\frac{3}{8} \cdot 5 =$ _____

15. $\frac{2}{3} \cdot 13 =$ _____ **16.** $\frac{5}{12} \cdot 18 =$ _____ **17.** $\frac{5}{9} \cdot 12 =$ _____

Remembering

Compare.

1. $\frac{5}{6}$ ◯ $\frac{5}{7}$

2. $\frac{1}{5}$ ◯ $\frac{1}{4}$

3. $\frac{8}{10}$ ◯ $\frac{6}{8}$

4. $\frac{6}{7}$ ◯ $\frac{7}{8}$

5. $\frac{2}{3}$ ◯ $\frac{3}{4}$

6. $\frac{8}{9}$ ◯ $\frac{6}{7}$

Compare.

7. 0.54 ◯ 0.65

8. 0.207 ◯ 0.342

9. 0.5 ◯ 0.47

10. 0.76 ◯ 0.67

11. 0.22 ◯ 0.41

12. 0.6 ◯ 0.06

Multiply.

13. $\frac{4}{5} \cdot 20 =$ _____

14. $\frac{2}{3} \cdot 21 =$ _____

15. $\frac{5}{8} \cdot 24 =$ _____

16. $\frac{1}{9} \cdot 36 =$ _____

17. $\frac{3}{4} \cdot 16 =$ _____

18. $\frac{2}{7} \cdot 14 =$ _____

19. $\frac{3}{12} \cdot 24 =$ _____

20. $\frac{8}{10} \cdot 80 =$ _____

21. $\frac{3}{9} \cdot 45 =$ _____

22. **Stretch Your Thinking** Write a multiplication equation
    using one whole number and one fraction that have
    a product of $\frac{18}{8}$.

    _____

Multiplication with Fractional Solutions

Homework

Tanith is using a number line to find $\frac{3}{4} \cdot \frac{2}{5}$. This is her work so far:

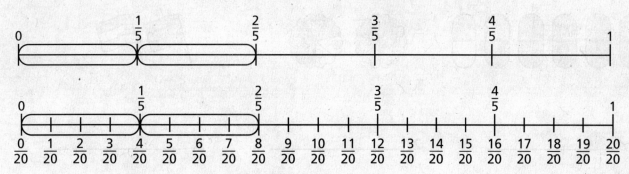

1. Explain Tanith's work so far to someone at home.

2. Finish Tanith's work by circling $\frac{3}{4}$ of each
circled fifth. How many 20ths did you circle altogether? _____

What is $\frac{3}{4} \cdot \frac{2}{5}$? _____

3. Use the number line to find $\frac{2}{3} \cdot \frac{5}{6}$.
Label all the parts above and below. _____

0 ├──────┼──────┼──────┼──────┼──────┼──────┤ 1

Solve.   *Show your work.*

4. Four friends at a party popped $\frac{3}{4}$ of a bag of popcorn.
They ate half of what was popped. What fraction of the
popcorn in the bag did they eat?

_____

5. Ashley brought $\frac{7}{8}$ gallon of lemonade to the party.
Her friends drank $\frac{2}{3}$ of it. How many gallons of
lemonade did they drink?

_____

Multiply. You do not need to simplify.

6. $\frac{2}{7} \cdot \frac{1}{3} =$ _____

7. $\frac{4}{9} \cdot \frac{2}{9} =$ _____

8. $\frac{1}{8} \cdot \frac{5}{6} =$ _____

9. $\frac{2}{7} \cdot 12 =$ _____

10. $\frac{4}{5} \cdot \frac{2}{3} =$ _____

11. $\frac{1}{7} \cdot \frac{3}{5} =$ _____

12. $\frac{9}{10} \cdot \frac{1}{2} =$ _____

13. $\frac{5}{12} \cdot 3 =$ _____

14. $\frac{5}{6} \cdot \frac{1}{6} =$ _____

Name _____ **Date** _____

Remembering

Name the mixed number shown by the shaded parts.

1. _____   2. _____   3. _____

Add.

4. $454 + 0.65 =$ _____   5. $80.55 + 0.91 =$ _____   6. $31.78 \text{ m} + 6.2 \text{ m} =$ _____

7. Show $\frac{1}{3}$ of 7 on the number line.

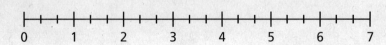

8. Write $\frac{1}{3}$ of 7 as a fraction. _____

9. Write $\frac{1}{3}$ of 7 as a mixed number. _____

10. **Stretch Your Thinking** Solve for the unknown fraction.
    Then divide and shade an area model to show the
    equation. $\frac{2}{5} \cdot \, ? = \frac{10}{30}$.

_____

Multiply a Fraction by a Fraction

Homework

Multiply. Simplify first if you can.

1. $\dfrac{2}{5} \cdot \dfrac{6}{7} =$ _____

2. $\dfrac{4}{9} \cdot \dfrac{1}{8} =$ _____

3. $\dfrac{5}{24} \cdot \dfrac{8}{15} =$ _____

4. $\dfrac{2}{17} \cdot \dfrac{8}{1} =$ _____

5. $\dfrac{3}{4} \cdot \dfrac{12}{25} =$ _____

6. $\dfrac{5}{7} \cdot \dfrac{3}{8} =$ _____

7. $\dfrac{3}{10} \cdot \dfrac{2}{3} =$ _____

8. $\dfrac{5}{16} \cdot \dfrac{2}{25} =$ _____

9. $\dfrac{4}{35} \cdot \dfrac{7}{12} =$ _____

10. $\dfrac{5}{6} \cdot \dfrac{7}{1} =$ _____

11. $\dfrac{7}{9} \cdot \dfrac{6}{49} =$ _____

12. $\dfrac{7}{8} \cdot \dfrac{2}{3} =$ _____

13. Which fraction is not equivalent to the others?

$\dfrac{3}{15}$ $\dfrac{2}{10}$ $\dfrac{1}{5}$ $\dfrac{9}{45}$ $\dfrac{10}{50}$ $\dfrac{6}{40}$ $\dfrac{7}{35}$ $\dfrac{100}{500}$

Solve.   *Show your work*

14. In the town zoo, $\dfrac{3}{28}$ of the animals are birds. Of the birds, $\dfrac{4}{15}$ are birds of prey. What fraction of the animals at the zoo are birds of prey?

_____

15. Tuesday at the zoo, $\dfrac{5}{12}$ of the visitors were adults. Of these adults, $\dfrac{3}{10}$ were men. What fraction of the people who visited the zoo on Tuesday were men?

_____

16. On Tuesday, $\dfrac{14}{25}$ of the souvenirs purchased at the zoo gift shop were stuffed animals. Of the stuffed animals purchased, $\dfrac{10}{21}$ were bears. What fraction of the souvenirs purchased at the zoo gift shop on Tuesday were stuffed bears?

_____

Remembering

Add or subtract.

1. $1\frac{4}{5} + 5\frac{2}{5}$

2. $5\frac{1}{6} + 3\frac{5}{6}$

3. $1\frac{2}{3} - \frac{1}{3}$

4. $\frac{3}{4} + \frac{5}{4}$

5. $7\frac{8}{9} - 3\frac{5}{9}$

6. $6 - 4\frac{1}{2}$

Subtract.

7. $31{,}763 - 6.51 =$

8. $132.76 - 87.24 =$

9. $968.29 - 217.5 =$

_____

_____

_____

10. Use the number line to find $\frac{3}{4} \cdot \frac{2}{5}$. Label all the parts above and below.

$\frac{3}{4} \cdot \frac{2}{5} =$ _____

0 ├─────────────────────────────────────┤ 1

11. **Stretch Your Thinking** Write a word problem that will use the equation $\frac{2}{6} \cdot \frac{8}{10} = x$ in order to solve. Then simplify and multiply to solve.

_____

_____

_____

_____

Homework

Find each product by first rewriting each mixed number as a fraction.

1. $\frac{3}{7} \cdot 2\frac{1}{2} =$ _____

2. $1\frac{7}{10} \cdot 5 =$ _____

3. $2\frac{2}{3} \cdot 4\frac{1}{5} =$ _____

4. $5\frac{1}{3} \cdot \frac{3}{8} =$ _____

5. $\frac{5}{9} \cdot 1\frac{2}{5} =$ _____

6. $12 \cdot 2\frac{3}{4} =$ _____

7. $3\frac{1}{2} \cdot 3\frac{1}{2} =$ _____

8. $\frac{1}{9} \cdot 3\frac{9}{10} =$ _____

Solve.

Show your work.

9. The bottom of Zeyda's jewelry box is a rectangle with length $5\frac{3}{8}$ inches and width $3\frac{1}{4}$ inches. What is the area of the bottom of the jewelry box?

_____

10. The Patel family went apple picking. The number of red apples they picked was $2\frac{2}{9}$ times the number of green apples they picked. If they picked 45 green apples, how many red apples did they pick?

_____

11. The art museum is $8\frac{1}{2}$ miles from Alison's house. Alison has ridden her bike $\frac{2}{3}$ of the way there so far. How far has she gone?

_____

Name _____ Date _____

Remembering

Add.

1. $\dfrac{3}{8} + \dfrac{1}{6}$

2. $\dfrac{1}{5} + \dfrac{3}{4}$

3. $\dfrac{5}{6} + \dfrac{1}{8}$

4. $\dfrac{1}{3} + \dfrac{2}{7}$

5. $\dfrac{2}{3} + \dfrac{1}{9}$

6. $\dfrac{4}{5} + \dfrac{1}{10}$

Use the Commutative Property to solve for _n_.

7. $55{,}207 + 87{,}331 = 87{,}331 + n$

$n = $ _____

8. $48.76 + 20.08 = 20.08 + n$

$n = $ _____

Multiply. Simplify first if you can.

9. $\dfrac{2}{3} \cdot \dfrac{3}{4} = $ _____

10. $\dfrac{7}{10} \cdot \dfrac{6}{7} = $ _____

11. $\dfrac{3}{5} \cdot \dfrac{5}{6} = $ _____

12. $\dfrac{5}{6} \cdot \dfrac{12}{25} = $ _____

13. $\dfrac{1}{2} \cdot \dfrac{4}{7} = $ _____

14. $\dfrac{2}{9} \cdot \dfrac{3}{8} = $ _____

15. **Stretch Your Thinking** Complete the mixed number equation
that is represented by the area model.

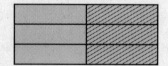 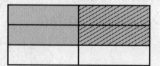

$\dfrac{1}{2} \cdot$ _____ $= $ _____

Multiply Mixed Numbers

Homework

Solve.

1. $\frac{3}{4} \cdot \frac{1}{8}$

2. $\frac{2}{3} - \frac{1}{9}$

3. $\frac{1}{10} + \frac{1}{5}$

4. $\frac{2}{7} \cdot 12$

5. $\frac{1}{5} + \frac{2}{3}$

6. $\frac{1}{4} + \frac{3}{8}$

7. $\frac{5}{7} \cdot \frac{5}{6}$

8. $\frac{11}{12} + 3$

9. $\frac{4}{9} - \frac{2}{9}$

10. $\frac{1}{3} \cdot \frac{1}{8}$

11. $\frac{7}{8} \cdot \frac{3}{4}$

12. $10 - \frac{1}{9}$

Solve.   *Show your work.*

13. Rodrigo's fish bowl holds $\frac{7}{8}$ gallon of water. It is now $\frac{1}{2}$ full. How much water is in it?

_____

14. Kenya jumped $7\frac{1}{6}$ feet. Janet jumped $6\frac{1}{3}$ feet. How much farther did Kenya jump?

_____

15. A group of hikers walked $8\frac{7}{10}$ miles to Caribou Cave and then $5\frac{1}{5}$ miles to Silver Stream. How far did they walk altogether?

_____

16. A recipe calls for $\frac{3}{4}$ cup of flour. Estevan wants to make $\frac{1}{3}$ of the recipe. How much flour will he need?

_____

17. A truck was carrying $2\frac{1}{8}$ tons of sand. When it arrived, only $1\frac{1}{2}$ tons of sand were left. How much sand was lost along the way?

_____

Name _____ **Date** _____

Remembering

Subtract.

1. $\frac{3}{4} - \frac{1}{6}$

2. $\frac{2}{9} - \frac{1}{10}$

3. $\frac{7}{8} - \frac{1}{4}$

4. $\frac{6}{7} - \frac{1}{3}$

5. $\frac{4}{5} - \frac{2}{3}$

6. $\frac{1}{2} - \frac{1}{8}$

Estimate each sum or difference.

7. $6.759 + 2.099$ _____

8. $\$44.25 - \$21.76$ _____

9. $14.6 + 2.4$ _____

Find each product by first rewriting each mixed number as a fraction.

10. $\frac{5}{8} \cdot 3\frac{1}{3} =$ _____

11. $4\frac{3}{5} \cdot 5 =$ _____

12. $1\frac{2}{5} \cdot 3\frac{4}{9} =$ _____

13. $6\frac{1}{5} \cdot \frac{5}{8} =$ _____

14. **Stretch Your Thinking** Give an example that shows how to use the Distributive Property to multiply a number by a sum. All of the numbers you use should be mixed numbers or fractions.

_____

_____

Relate Fraction Operations

Complete each fraction box.

1.

$\frac{7}{8}$ and $\frac{3}{4}$	
>	$\frac{7}{8} > \frac{3}{4}$ or $\frac{7}{8} > \frac{6}{8}$
+	
−	
·	

2.

$\frac{1}{2}$ and $\frac{3}{5}$	
>	
+	
−	
·	

Solve.

Show your work.

3. The Eagle Trucking Company must deliver $\frac{7}{8}$ ton of cement blocks and $\frac{5}{8}$ ton of bricks to one place. How much will this load weigh?

_____

4. A truck carried $3\frac{1}{3}$ tons of sand, but lost $\frac{1}{4}$ ton along the way. How many tons of sand were delivered?

_____

5. The trucking company also needs to deliver $1\frac{2}{3}$ tons of oak logs and $1\frac{7}{12}$ tons of maple logs. Which load weighs more?

_____

6. In a load of $\frac{3}{4}$ ton of steel rods, $\frac{1}{8}$ of them are bent. How many tons of steel rods are bent?

_____

7. The company delivered $1\frac{3}{5}$ tons of bricks to one building site. They delivered $2\frac{1}{2}$ times this much to a second site. What was the weight of the load the company delivered to the second site?

_____

Name _____ **Date** _____

Remembering

Multiply.

1. 2,548
    ×   5

2. 21
    × 45

3. 3,015
    ×   6

4. 33
    × 4

5. 65
    × 87

6. 215
    ×   9

Find each product by first rewriting each mixed number as a fraction.

7. $4\frac{4}{9} \cdot 2\frac{2}{3} =$ _____

8. $6\frac{1}{5} \cdot 10 =$ _____

9. $3\frac{5}{6} \cdot \frac{12}{13} =$ _____

10. $5\frac{1}{3} \cdot \frac{3}{5} =$ _____

Solve.

11. $\frac{6}{7} - \frac{2}{7}$

12. $\frac{4}{9} + \frac{2}{3}$

13. $\frac{2}{3} \cdot \frac{9}{10}$

14. $\frac{3}{5} \cdot \frac{5}{8}$

15. $8 - \frac{1}{7}$

16. $\frac{1}{6} + \frac{3}{8}$

17. **Stretch Your Thinking** Write and solve a word problem
that requires multiplying two mixed numbers.

_____

_____

_____

_____

       Solve Real World Problems

Homework

Predict whether the product will be greater than, less than, or equal to the second factor. Then compute the product.

1. $\frac{4}{5} \cdot 6 = x$

Predict: $x \bigcirc 6$

Compute: $x =$ _____

2. $1\frac{1}{9} \cdot 6 = x$

Predict: $x \bigcirc 6$

Compute: $x =$ _____

3. $\frac{10}{10} \cdot 6 = x$

Predict: $x \bigcirc 6$

Compute: $x =$ _____

4. $\frac{2}{2} \cdot \frac{5}{6} = x$

Predict: $x \bigcirc \frac{5}{6}$

Compute: $x =$ _____

5. $\frac{5}{6} \cdot \frac{5}{6} = x$

Predict: $x \bigcirc \frac{5}{6}$

Compute: $x =$ _____

6. $1\frac{1}{3} \cdot \frac{5}{6} = x$

Predict: $x \bigcirc \frac{5}{6}$

Compute: $x =$ _____

Solve.

Show your work.

7. James is $1\frac{3}{7}$ times as tall as his brother. His brother is $3\frac{1}{2}$ feet tall.

Is James's height more or less than $3\frac{1}{2}$ feet?

_____

How tall is James?

_____

8. South Middle School has 750 students. North Middle School has $\frac{13}{15}$ times as many students as South.

Does North Middle School have more or fewer than 750 students?

_____

How many students attend North Middle School?

_____

Remembering

Perry measured the foot length of four friends for a science fair experiment. Then, he made a bar graph to display his results.

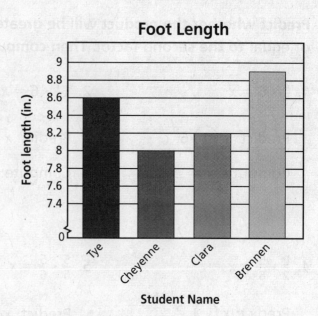

Foot Length

1. How much longer is Brennen's foot than Clara's foot?

   _____

2. What is the difference between the longest foot and the shortest foot?

   _____

Solve.

3. $\frac{7}{8} \cdot \frac{4}{9}$

4. $11 - \frac{3}{4}$

5. $\frac{4}{5} + \frac{7}{10}$

6. $\frac{9}{12} - \frac{5}{12}$

7. $\frac{7}{15} + \frac{2}{3}$

8. $\frac{5}{6} \cdot \frac{9}{11}$

Complete each fraction box.

$\frac{7}{12}$ and $\frac{5}{6}$	
>	
+	
−	
·	

$\frac{4}{5}$ and $\frac{2}{3}$	
>	
+	
−	
·	

9. **Stretch Your Thinking** Write two multiplication equations using fractions and mixed numbers. Write one equation that will have a product greater than the first factor. Then write another equation that will have a product less than the first factor.

_____

Divide

1. $5 \div 6 =$ _____ .

2. $9 \div \frac{1}{5} =$ _____

3. $33 \div 30 =$ _____

4. $8 \div \frac{1}{6} =$ _____

5. $3 \div 10 =$ _____

6. $4 \div \frac{1}{9} =$ _____

7. $100 \div \frac{1}{6} =$ _____

8. $1 \div 100 =$ _____

9. $\frac{1}{5} \div 8 =$ _____

10. $\frac{1}{8} \div 7 =$ _____

11. $\frac{1}{2} \div 9 =$ _____

12. $\frac{1}{3} \div 5 =$ _____

Solve.

Show your work.

13. Alexander is dividing oranges into eighths. He has 5 oranges. How many eighths will he have?

_____

14. Carrie has 32 ounces of ice cream to divide equally among 10 people. How much ice cream will each person get?

_____

15. Nayati wants to swim 50 miles this school year. She plans to swim $\frac{1}{4}$ mile each day. How many days will it take her to swim 50 miles?

_____

16. Eric has $\frac{1}{3}$ of a watermelon to share equally with 3 friends. How much will each person get?

_____

17. A gardener needs to pack 16 pounds of beans into 20 bags. He wants all the bags to weigh about the same. About how much will each bag weigh?

_____

Remembering

Add or subtract.

1. $2\frac{3}{4}$
   $-\ 1\frac{5}{8}$
   _____

2. $4\frac{2}{3}$
   $+\ 1\frac{5}{9}$
   _____

3. $10\frac{1}{2}$
   $-\ 3\frac{4}{5}$
   _____

4. 7
   $-\ 2\frac{1}{6}$
   _____

5. $3\frac{2}{5}$
   $+\ 4\frac{5}{6}$
   _____

6. $8\frac{1}{3}$
   $+\ 1\frac{3}{4}$
   _____

Complete each fraction box.

7.

$\frac{2}{5}$ and $\frac{2}{7}$	
>	
+	
−	
·	

8.

$\frac{5}{6}$ and $\frac{6}{7}$	
>	
+	
−	
·	

Predict whether the product will be greater than, less than, or equal to the second factor. Then compute the product.

9. $\frac{2}{3} \cdot 5 = x$

Predict: $x \bigcirc 5$

Compute: $x = $ _____

10. $\frac{3}{3} \cdot 5 = x$

Predict: $x \bigcirc 5$

Compute: $x = $ _____

11. $1\frac{1}{6} \cdot 5 = x$

Predict: $x \bigcirc 5$

Compute: $x = $ _____

12. **Stretch Your Thinking** Draw a diagram to show how many twelfths there are in 3. Describe a situation in which you would need to know how many twelfths there are in 3.

_____

_____

_____

When Dividing Is Also Multiplying

1. Consider the division problem $\frac{1}{2} \div 3$.

   Describe a situation this division could represent.

   _____

   _____

   Draw a diagram to represent the division. Then find the solution.

Write an equation. Then solve.   *Show your work.*

2. A rectangle has an area of 12 square feet and a length of 5 feet. What is its width?

   _____

3. A tortoise must walk $\frac{1}{12}$ mile to visit a friend. He plans to break the journey into four equal parts with breaks in between. How long will each part of his journey be?

   _____

4. Harry worked 7 hours last week. This is $\frac{1}{3}$ as many hours as Aidan worked. How many hours did Aidan work?

   _____

5. Lin is a camp counselor. She is making small bags of trail mix for campers to take on a hike. She has 2 pounds of raisins and is putting $\frac{1}{8}$ pound in each bag. How many bags can she fill before she runs out of raisins?

   _____

6. Mr. Ramirez bought $\frac{1}{4}$ pounds of cashews. He divided the cashews equally among his three children. How much did each child get?

   _____

Remembering

Solve Division Problems

Add or subtract.

1. $1\frac{1}{8}$
   $+ 4\frac{2}{3}$

2. $6\frac{1}{4}$
   $- 4\frac{5}{6}$

3. $9\frac{1}{3}$
   $+ 7\frac{8}{9}$

4. $5\frac{2}{7}$
   $+ 5\frac{11}{14}$

5. 4
   $- 2\frac{2}{5}$

6. $6\frac{5}{8}$
   $+ 3\frac{1}{2}$

Predict whether the product will be greater than, less than, or equal to the second factor. Then compute the product.

7. $\frac{5}{5} \cdot 9 = x$

   Predict: $x \bigcirc 9$

   Compute: $x =$ _____

8. $\frac{7}{8} \cdot 9 = x$

   Predict: $x \bigcirc 9$

   Compute: $x =$ _____

9. $1\frac{3}{5} \cdot 9 = x$

   Predict: $x \bigcirc 9$

   Compute: $x =$ _____

10. $1\frac{1}{2} \cdot \frac{4}{5} = x$

   Predict: $x \bigcirc \frac{4}{5}$

   Compute: $x =$ _____

11. $\frac{6}{6} \cdot \frac{4}{5} = x$

   Predict: $x \bigcirc \frac{4}{5}$

   Compute: $x =$ _____

12. $\frac{2}{5} \cdot \frac{4}{5} = x$

   Predict: $x \bigcirc \frac{4}{5}$

   Compute: $x =$ _____

Divide.

13. $6 \div \frac{1}{4} =$ _____

14. $2 \div 3 =$ _____

15. $10 \div 3 =$ _____

16. $200 \div \frac{1}{4} =$ _____

17. $\frac{1}{4} \div 8 =$ _____

18. $\frac{1}{7} \div 6 =$ _____

19. **Stretch Your Thinking** Harrison is playing a board game that has a path of 100 spaces. After his first turn, he is $\frac{1}{5}$ of the way along the spaces. On his second turn, he moves $\frac{1}{4}$ fewer spaces than he moved on his first turn. On his third turn, he moves $1\frac{1}{4}$ times as many spaces than he moved on his first turn. What space is he on after three turns?

_____

Solve Division Problems

Solve.

1. $5 \cdot \frac{1}{3} =$ _____

2. $5 \div \frac{1}{3} =$ _____

3. $\frac{1}{8} \div 2 =$ _____

4. $27 \div 10 =$ _____

5. $5 \div \frac{1}{100} =$ _____

6. $12 \cdot \frac{1}{9} =$ _____

7. $\frac{3}{5} \cdot \frac{10}{27} =$ _____

8. $16 \div \frac{1}{4} =$ _____

9. $\frac{1}{5} \div 10 =$ _____

10. $10 \div \frac{1}{5} =$ _____

11. $\frac{1}{8} \cdot 14 =$ _____

12. $18 \div 20 =$ _____

Tell whether you need to multiply or divide. Then solve.   *Show your work.*

13. A dime weighs about $\frac{1}{12}$ ounce. Jody has 1 pound
(16 ounces) of dimes. About many dimes does she have?

_____

14. Maddie has 180 coins. Of these coins, $\frac{1}{12}$ are dimes.
About how many dimes does she have?

_____

15. A rectangle has length 3 feet and width $\frac{1}{4}$ foot. What is the
area of the rectangle?

_____

16. A rectangle has area 3 square feet and width $\frac{1}{2}$ foot.
What is the length of the rectangle?

_____

17. Nisha wants to study 5 hours for the spelling bee. If she
studies $\frac{1}{3}$ hour per night, how many nights will she
have to study?

_____

Remembering

Multiply.

1. $134 \cdot 5 =$ _____

2. $44 \cdot 21 =$ _____

3. $7 \cdot 57 =$ _____

4. $4{,}507 \cdot 3 =$ _____

5. $36 \cdot 76 =$ _____

6. $1{,}928 \cdot 6 =$ _____

Divide.

7. $\frac{1}{9} \div 2 =$ _____

8. $100 \div \frac{1}{3} =$ _____

9. $\frac{1}{5} \div 4 =$ _____

10. $4 \div 5 =$ _____

11. $12 \div 5 =$ _____

12. $8 \div \frac{1}{7} =$ _____

Write an equation. Then solve.   *Show your work.*

13. Marc is running 5 kilometers at track practice. He decides to break the run into 3 equal lengths. How long will each length be?

_____

14. **Stretch Your Thinking** Using a whole number and a fraction as factors, write a multiplication equation with a product less than the whole number factor. Draw a picture to show how the product is less than the whole number factor.

_____

Distinguishing Multiplication from Division

Homework

Solve.

Show your work.

1. Dan's Ice Cream comes in cartons of two sizes. The large carton holds $4\frac{1}{2}$ pounds. The small carton holds $1\frac{3}{4}$ pounds less. How much ice cream does the small carton hold?

   _____

2. Mac picked four baskets of blueberries. The weights of the berries in pounds are given below. Order the weights from lightest to heaviest.

   $\frac{5}{4}$ $\frac{9}{10}$ $\frac{4}{5}$ $\frac{13}{20}$

   _____

3. Four cones of Dan's Ice Cream hold $\frac{1}{2}$ pound. How much ice cream does each cone hold?

   _____

4. If a dish of ice cream holds $\frac{1}{4}$ pound, how many dishes can you get from a $4\frac{1}{2}$-pound carton of Dan's Ice Cream?

   _____

Solve. Give your answer in simplest form.

5. $3 \div \frac{1}{5} =$ _____

6. $1\frac{3}{4} + \frac{11}{16} =$ _____

7. $\frac{9}{14} \cdot 2\frac{1}{3} =$ _____

8. $2\frac{3}{5} \cdot 6 =$ _____

9. $\frac{1}{3} + \frac{3}{5} =$ _____

10. $\frac{5}{6} + \frac{8}{9} =$ _____

11. $\frac{1}{8} \div 4 =$ _____

12. $\frac{2}{5} - \frac{1}{10} =$ _____

13. $3\frac{5}{7} - 1\frac{1}{2} =$ _____

14. $\frac{7}{8} \cdot \frac{2}{7} =$ _____

Name _____ **Date** _____

Remembering

Use benchmarks of 0, $\frac{1}{2}$, and 1 to estimate the sum or difference. Then find the actual sum or difference.

1. $\frac{5}{10} + \frac{4}{9}$

   Estimate: _____

   Sum: _____

2. $\frac{13}{14} - \frac{3}{7}$

   Estimate: _____

   Difference: _____

3. $\frac{8}{9} - \frac{7}{8}$

   Estimate: _____

   Difference: _____

4. $\frac{13}{14} + \frac{3}{4}$

   Estimate: _____

   Sum: _____

Write an equation. Then solve.   _Show your work._

5. A rectangle has an area of 20 square feet and a length of 6 feet. What is its width?

   _____

6. Bailey attends gymnastics practice for 8 hours each week. This is $\frac{1}{4}$ the number of hours that the gym is open for practice. How many hours is the gym open for practice?

   _____

Solve.

7. $\frac{1}{4} \div 3 =$ _____

8. $\frac{1}{4} \cdot 3 =$ _____

9. $14 \cdot \frac{1}{6} =$ _____

10. **Stretch Your Thinking** How is solving $\frac{1}{8} \div 5$ different from solving $\frac{1}{8} \cdot 5$?

   _____

   _____

   _____

   _____

Review Operations with Fractions

Homework

These graphs show the instruments in two different high school marching bands.

Carter School Marching Band

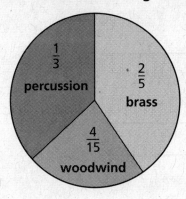

Reagan School Marching Band

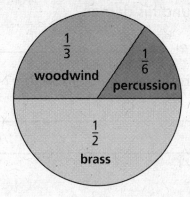

Solve. Use the circle graphs.   *Show your work.*

1. The Reagan School Marching Band has three percussion musicians. How many musicians altogether are in the band?

   _____

2. There are 30 musicians in the Carter School Marching Band. How many of them play brass instruments?

   _____

Suppose both bands decide to combine and perform as one band.

3. What fraction of the band members will play a brass instrument?

   _____

4. What fraction of the band members will play a percussion instrument?

   _____

5. What fraction of the band members will play a woodwind instrument?

   _____

Remembering

Solve. Explain how you know your answer is reasonable. *Show your work.*

1. James's garden has a length of $12\frac{1}{4}$ feet and a width of $9\frac{2}{3}$ feet. What length of fencing will he need to surround his garden?

   Answer: _____

   Why is the answer reasonable?

   _____

   _____

Solve.

2. $\frac{1}{11} \div 3 =$ _____

3. $6 \div \frac{1}{3} =$ _____

4. $\frac{2}{3} \cdot \frac{5}{7} =$ _____

5. $\frac{1}{12} \div 5 =$ _____

6. $7 \cdot \frac{1}{8} =$ _____

7. $\frac{1}{5} \cdot 12 =$ _____

Solve. *Show your work.*

8. Kayla packs 4 boxes that weigh $\frac{1}{6}$ pound altogether. What does each box weigh?

   _____

9. Mrs. Blackwell put $4\frac{2}{3}$ grams on the scale during a lab in science class. Then, she added $2\frac{5}{6}$ grams to the scale. How many grams are on the scale in all?

   _____

10. **Stretch Your Thinking** If you start with 1 and repeatedly multiply by $\frac{1}{2}$, will you reach 0? Explain why or why not.

    _____

    _____

    _____

Focus on Mathematical Practices

Homework

Solve.

1. 40	2. 400	3. 400	4. 4,000
× 2	× 2	× 20	× 2

5. 80	6. 800	7. 800	8. 80
× 60	× 60	× 6	× 600

9. 70	10. 900	11. 800	12. 6,000
× 20	× 40	× 70	× 7

Solve.

Show your work.

13. A tortoise walks 27 miles in a year. At this rate, how many miles will this tortoise walk in 10 years?

_____

14. If the tortoise lives to be 100 years old, how many miles will it walk during its lifetime?

_____

15. Every month, Paolo earns $40 for walking his neighbor's dog after school. How much does he earn from this job in one year?

_____

16. There are 60 seconds in a minute and 60 minutes in an hour. How many seconds are there in an hour?

_____

17. An elephant eats about 2,500 pounds of food in 10 days. About how much food does an elephant eat in 1,000 days?

_____

Remembering

Write the multiplier or divisor for each pair of equivalent fractions.

1. $\frac{4}{5} = \frac{12}{15}$

   Multiplier = _____

2. $\frac{25}{60} = \frac{5}{12}$

   Divisor = _____

3. $\frac{12}{20} = \frac{3}{5}$

   Divisor = _____

4. $\frac{2}{3} = \frac{20}{30}$

   Multiplier = _____

5. $\frac{27}{36} = \frac{3}{4}$

   Divisor = _____

6. $\frac{1}{8} = \frac{7}{56}$

   Multiplier = _____

Solve.

7. Jordan shoots 100 3-point shots per basketball practice. She makes 44 of these shots. What decimal represents the number of shots she makes?

   _____

8. At a county fair, 9 people out of 1,000 earned a perfect score in a carnival game. What decimal represents the number of people who earned a perfect score?

   _____

Solve.

9. $\frac{1}{6} \cdot 60 =$ _____

10. $\frac{1}{3} \cdot 21 =$ _____

11. $\frac{1}{9}$ of 81 = _____

12. $\frac{1}{3} \cdot 24 =$ _____

13. $\frac{1}{5}$ of 60 = _____

14. $\frac{1}{8} \cdot 16 =$ _____

15. **Stretch Your Thinking** Using a multiple of ten for at least one factor, write an equation with a product that has four zeros.

   _____

Solve.

1. 60 × 40	**2.** 70 × 40	**3.** 700 × 60	
4. 300 × 50	**5.** 40 × 50	**6.** 900 × 30	
7. 400 × 80	**8.** 200 × 50	**9.** 300 × 200	

The table shows the sizes of Farmer Reuben's fields.
Use the table and a separate sheet of paper to help you
answer each question.

	Corn Field	400 feet by 60 feet
	Wheat Field	700 feet by 200 feet
	Barley Field	200 feet by 200 feet

10. What is the area of the corn field?

_____

11. What is the area of the wheat field?

_____

12. What is the area of the barley field?

_____

13. How many square feet of land did Farmer Reuben
plant in all?

_____

Name _____ Date _____

Remembering

Compare.

1. $\frac{5}{8}$ ◯ $\frac{5}{7}$

2. $\frac{3}{4}$ ◯ $\frac{5}{6}$

3. $\frac{9}{10}$ ◯ $\frac{8}{9}$

4. $\frac{3}{8}$ ◯ $\frac{5}{8}$

5. $\frac{1}{7}$ ◯ $\frac{1}{8}$

6. $\frac{4}{5}$ ◯ $\frac{4}{7}$

Multiply.

7. $\frac{5}{6} \cdot 36 =$ _____

8. $\frac{1}{8} \cdot 40 =$ _____

9. $\frac{2}{5} \cdot 60 =$ _____

10. $\frac{2}{3} \cdot 33 =$ _____

11. $\frac{3}{4} \cdot 36 =$ _____

12. $\frac{2}{9} \cdot 45 =$ _____

Solve.

13. 50
     $\times\ 2$

14. 500
     $\times\ 2$

15. 5,000
     $\times\ 2$

16. 60
     $\times\ 40$

17. 600
     $\times\ 40$

18. 600
     $\times\ 4$

19. **Stretch Your Thinking** Explain how to predict the number of zeros in the product for the expression 600 · 500.

_____

_____

_____

Patterns With Fives and Zeros

Homework

Solve the first problem with Place Value Sections.
Solve the other problems using any method you like.
Use a separate sheet of paper.

1.

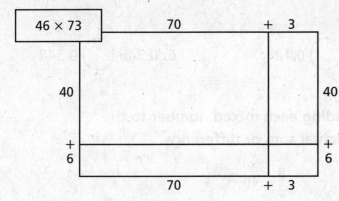

2. 84
    × 19

3. 67
    × 53

4. 91
    × 28

Solve.   *Show your work.*

5. Kamini needs to know the area of her yard so that she can
   buy the right amount of grass seed. The yard is 26 feet by
   19 feet. What is the area of Kamini's yard in square feet?

   _____

6. A restaurant has 16 crates of juice. Each crate holds 12 gallons
   of juice. How many gallons of juice are there altogether?

   _____

7. Mr. Jackson is taking 23 students to see a movie. Tickets
   for the movie cost 75 cents. How much money will
   Mr. Jackson spend on student tickets?

   _____

8. There are usually 20 school days in a month. Grace has band
   practice for 60 minutes every day after school. How many
   minutes does she usually practice each month?

   _____

Remembering

Compare. Write > (greater than) or < (less than).

1. 0.7 ◯ 0.71

2. 0.2 ◯ 0.02

3. 0.76 ◯ 0.68

4. 0.31 ◯ 0.43

5. 0.21 ◯ 0.12

6. 0.346 ◯ 0.348

Estimate the sum or difference by rounding each mixed number to the nearest whole number. Then find the actual sum or difference.

7. $2\frac{1}{8} + 6\frac{6}{7}$

Estimate: _____

Sum: _____

8. $7\frac{9}{10} - 4\frac{1}{9}$

Estimate: _____

Difference: _____

9. $5\frac{7}{8} - 1\frac{1}{10}$

Estimate: _____

Difference: _____

10. $6\frac{3}{8} + 7\frac{2}{5}$

Estimate: _____

Sum: _____

Multiply.

11. 80
    × 60

12. 200
    × 30

13. 400
    × 40

14. 600
    × 50

15. 500
    × 10

16. 300
    × 90

17. **Stretch Your Thinking** Explain how to check multiplication using addition or division. Include an example in your explanation.

_____

_____

_____

Sharing Methods for Multiplication

Solve. Use any method.

1. 78
   × 26

2. 93
   × 42

3. 39
   × 84

4. 56
   × 71

The table shows how many newspapers are
delivered each week by three paper carriers.
Use the table to answer the questions.
Use 1 year = 52 weeks.

Papers Delivered Each Week

Jameel	93
Clare	97
Mason	98

Show your work.

5. How many papers does Jameel deliver in a year?

   _____

6. How many papers does Clare deliver in a year?

   _____

7. How could you find how many papers Mason delivers in
   a year without doing any multiplication? What is the answer?

   _____

   _____

   _____

Solve.

8. Ray needs to know the area of his floor so he can buy the
   right amount of carpet. The floor is 21 feet by 17 feet.
   What is the area of the floor?

   _____

9. Maria is buying flowers. Each tray of flowers costs $24.
   If she buys 15 trays, what will the total cost be?

   _____

Remembering

Copy each exercise. Then subtract.

1. $9,000 - 865 =$ _____   **2.** $105.66 - 98.53 =$ _____   **3.** $45,688 - 5.65 =$ _____

Multiply. You do not need to simplify.

4. $\frac{5}{7} \cdot \frac{1}{3} =$ _____

5. $\frac{3}{5} \cdot \frac{1}{5} =$ _____

6. $\frac{1}{5} \cdot \frac{2}{7} =$ _____

7. $\frac{2}{3} \cdot 5 =$ _____

8. $\frac{3}{4} \cdot \frac{3}{4} =$ _____

9. $\frac{1}{2} \cdot \frac{5}{9} =$ _____

Solve the first problem with Place-Value Sections. Solve the other problems using any method you like.

10.

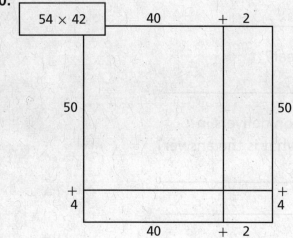

54 × 42	40	+ 2
50		50
+ 4		+ 4
	40	+ 2

11.   15
      $\times\ 42$

12.   65
      $\times\ 81$

13.   48
      $\times\ 24$

14. Stretch Your Thinking How is multiplying a 1-digit number and a 2-digit number the same as, and different from, multiplying two 2-digit numbers?

_____

_____

_____

_____

Multiply Two-Digit Numbers

Multiply.

1. 397
   × 9

2. 723
   × 7

3. 4,188
   × 3

4. 4,294
   × 4

5. 67
   × 82

6. 56
   × 49

7. 36
   × 29

8. 87
   × 71

9. 28
   × 27

10. 37
    × 54

11. 63
    × 91

12. 73
    × 35

13. 46
    × 83

14. 57
    × 75

15. 94
    × 47

16. 66
    × 86

Solve.

17. Jamal is building a bed for his dog. The dimensions of
    the bed are 27 inches by 36 inches. What is the area of
    the bottom of the bed?

    _____

18. Mr. Battle drives 9 miles to work every day. He works 5 days
    a week. How many miles does he travel to and from work
    over 52 weeks?

    _____

Name _____ **Date** _____

Remembering

Add or subtract.

1. $3\frac{3}{4}$
    $+ 2\frac{1}{8}$
    _____

2. $4\frac{1}{5}$
    $- 2\frac{3}{10}$
    _____

3. $5\frac{2}{5}$
    $+ 3\frac{1}{3}$
    _____

4. $6\frac{5}{6}$
    $+ 2\frac{5}{12}$
    _____

5. 10
    $- 2\frac{3}{5}$
    _____

6. $3\frac{2}{5}$
    $+ 1\frac{1}{15}$
    _____

Find each product by first rewriting each mixed number as a fraction.

7. $\frac{2}{9} \cdot 2\frac{2}{3} =$ _____

8. $1\frac{3}{5} \cdot 10 =$ _____

9. $4\frac{1}{4} \cdot 1\frac{1}{3} =$ _____

10. $2\frac{2}{5} \cdot \frac{3}{7} =$ _____

Solve. Use any method.

11. 64
     $\times\ 87$
     _____

12. 76
     $\times\ 35$
     _____

13. 53
     $\times\ 41$
     _____

14. 24
     $\times\ 72$
     _____

15. 19
     $\times\ 66$
     _____

16. 58
     $\times\ 36$
     _____

17. **Stretch Your Thinking** Explain how to use mental math to find the product of 64 and 25.

_____

_____

_____

Practice Multiplication

Homework

Solve.

1.	0.9	2.	0.6	3.	0.04	4.	0.05	5.	0.16
	× 7		× 80		× 9		× 70		× 7

6.	7.0	7.	0.09	8.	0.07	9.	0.17	10.	940
	× 8		× 30		× 60		× 81		× 0.2

11.	3.43	12.	0.29	13.	0.15	14.	1.57	15.	2.03
	× 7		× 86		× 196		× 52		× 121

Three runners started making a table for April to show how far they run every day, every week, and the entire month.

Show your work.

16. Finish the table for the runners.

Runner	Miles Per Day	Miles Per Week	Miles in April
Cedric	0.6	7 × 0.6 =	30 × 0.6 =
Shannon	2.4		
Regina	1.75		

17. Give the total miles in May for each runner below.

Cedric: _____ Shannon: _____ Regina: _____

_____ _____ _____

Remembering

Add.

1. $\dfrac{2}{7} + \dfrac{1}{5}$

2. $\dfrac{1}{3} + \dfrac{2}{5}$

3. $\dfrac{1}{3} + \dfrac{1}{8}$

4. $\dfrac{1}{2} + \dfrac{1}{5}$

5. $\dfrac{4}{5} + \dfrac{1}{6}$

6. $\dfrac{5}{8} + \dfrac{1}{10}$

Copy each exercise. Then add.

7. 46¢ + $3.48 =

_____

8. 0.23 m + 0.54 m =

_____

9. 33¢ + $11 =

_____

Multiply.

10. 458
× 3

11. 893
× 6

12. 6,236
× 7

13. 6,982
× 5

14. Stretch Your Thinking Marissa bought four bottles of water.
Each bottle of water was 95 cents. Write an equation with the
same product as the total cost but different factors.

_____

_____

Multiply Decimals with Whole Numbers

Homework

Solve.

1. $0.3 \times 0.6 =$ _____   **2.** $0.4 \times 0.07 =$ _____   **3.** $0.03 \times 0.8 =$ _____

4. $5 \times 0.07 =$ _____   **5.** $0.02 \times 0.3 =$ _____   **6.** $0.05 \times 0.9 =$ _____

7. $\begin{array}{r} 1.8 \\ \times\ \ 6 \\ \hline \end{array}$ **8.** $\begin{array}{r} 0.23 \\ \times\ \ 40 \\ \hline \end{array}$ **9.** $\begin{array}{r} 0.14 \\ \times\ 0.9 \\ \hline \end{array}$ **10.** $\begin{array}{r} 0.36 \\ \times\ 0.8 \\ \hline \end{array}$

11. $\begin{array}{r} 1.4 \\ \times\ 0.5 \\ \hline \end{array}$ **12.** $\begin{array}{r} 0.32 \\ \times\ 51 \\ \hline \end{array}$ **13.** $\begin{array}{r} 0.6 \\ \times\ 0.14 \\ \hline \end{array}$ **14.** $\begin{array}{r} 2.6 \\ \times\ 0.9 \\ \hline \end{array}$

Solve using mental math.

15. $82 \times 0.01 =$ _____   **16.** $385 \times 0.1 =$ _____   **17.** $2{,}194 \times 0.01 =$ _____

Solve.

18. Simon sold bottles of water at the marathon on
Saturday for $0.75 per bottle. He sold 43 bottles.
How much money did he earn?

_____

19. Lauren has 9.9 meters of ribbon. She is cutting it into
100 equal pieces. That is the same as multiplying 9.9 by 0.01.
How long will each piece of ribbon be?

_____

20. A furlong is a unit of measure used in horse racing.
Every year, horses race 10 furlongs in the Kentucky Derby.
One furlong is equal to 0.125 mile. How long is the
Kentucky Derby in miles?

_____

Name _____ **Date** _____

Remembering

Use the Distributive Property to rewrite each problem so it has only two factors. Then solve.

1. $(7 \times 200) + (7 \times 800) =$ _____

2. $(44 \times 3) + (56 \times 3) =$ _____

Multiply. Simplify first if you can.

3. $\frac{5}{8} \cdot \frac{6}{7} =$ _____

4. $\frac{1}{5} \cdot \frac{2}{9} =$ _____

5. $\frac{1}{2} \cdot \frac{4}{9} =$ _____

6. $\frac{2}{3} \cdot \frac{15}{16} =$ _____

7. $\frac{1}{8} \cdot \frac{6}{7} =$ _____

8. $\frac{9}{10} \cdot \frac{5}{6} =$ _____

Solve.

9.
$$\begin{array}{r} 0.7 \\ \times\ 6 \\ \hline \end{array}$$

10.
$$\begin{array}{r} 0.02 \\ \times\ 60 \\ \hline \end{array}$$

11.
$$\begin{array}{r} 0.15 \\ \times\ 34 \\ \hline \end{array}$$

12.
$$\begin{array}{r} 0.41 \\ \times\ 66 \\ \hline \end{array}$$

13.
$$\begin{array}{r} 1.24 \\ \times\ 6 \\ \hline \end{array}$$

14.
$$\begin{array}{r} 260 \\ \times\ 0.3 \\ \hline \end{array}$$

15. **Stretch Your Thinking** Explain where to place the decimal point in the product for the expression $0.5 \cdot 0.03$.

_____

_____

_____

_____

Multiply by Decimals

Homework

Solve.

1. 4.2 × 8.1	**2.** 9.4 × 6.3	**3.** 0.78 × 4.7	**4.** 0.05 × 3.7
5. 0.3 × 1.52	**6.** 0.80 × 3.8	**7.** 7.1 × 4.5	**8.** 2.4 × 0.64
9. 0.06 × 5.7	**10.** 9.9 × 6.6	**11.** 8.1 × 5.7	**12.** 0.07 × 24.3

Complete. Name the property used.

13. $(4.3 \times 6.2) - ($ _____ $\times 1.1) =$
$4.3 \times (6.2 - 1.1)$

14. $8.9 \times (5.3 \times 3.4) =$
$(8.9 \times$ _____ $) \times 3.4$

_____

_____

Solve.

15. Lester's car can go 15.4 miles on 1 gallon of gas. How far can he go on 0.7 gallon?

16. Clara wants to cover the top of her jewelry box. The top of the box is a rectangle with a length of 9.4 cm and a width of 8.3 cm. What is the total area she wants to cover?

_____

_____

Name _____

Date _____

Remembering

Solve. Explain how you know your answer is reasonable.

Show your work.

1. A rectangular sand box has a length of $5\frac{1}{3}$ feet and a width of $3\frac{3}{4}$ feet. What is its perimeter?

   Answer: _____

   Why is the answer reasonable?

   _____

   _____

Solve.

Show your work.

2. Kelly babysits for $5\frac{5}{6}$ hours on the weekend. This is $2\frac{1}{12}$ hours more than she babysits during the week. How many hours does she babysit during the week?

   _____

3. Lucas is making a recipe that requires $\frac{1}{4}$ cup of wheat flour and $1\frac{7}{8}$ cups of white flour. Altogether, how may cups of flour does the recipe require?

   _____

Solve.

4. $0.5 \times 0.4 =$ _____

5. $0.6 \times 0.09 =$ _____

6. $0.08 \times 0.3 =$ _____

7. $\begin{array}{r} 1.7 \\ \times\ \ 8 \\ \hline \end{array}$

8. $\begin{array}{r} 0.55 \\ \times\ \ 50 \\ \hline \end{array}$

9. $\begin{array}{r} 0.07 \\ \times\ 0.7 \\ \hline \end{array}$

10. **Stretch Your Thinking** Write a decimal equation that has a product of 3.15. (Do not use 1 as a factor.)

    _____

Multiply with Decimals Greater Than 1

Homework

Solve.

1. 4.8
× 100

2. 2.9
× 0.3

3. 0.56
× 20

4. 0.69
× 0.7

5. 2.6
× 3.4

6. 3.8
× 0.5

7. 1.5
× 4.9

8. 3.4
× 1.6

Complete the equations.

9. $0.7 \times 10^1 = $ _____

$0.7 \times 10^2 = $ _____

$0.7 \times 10^3 = $ _____

10. $0.98 \times 10^1 = $ _____

$0.98 \times 10^2 = $ _____

$0.98 \times 10^3 = $ _____

11. $5.63 \times 10^1 = $ _____

$5.63 \times 10^2 = $ _____

$5.63 \times 10^3 = $ _____

12. $3.7 \times 10^1 = $ _____

$3.7 \times 10^2 = $ _____

$3.7 \times $ _____ $ = 3,700$

13. $2.04 \times 10^1 = $ _____

$2.04 \times $ _____ $ = 204$

$2.04 \times 10^3 = $ _____

14. $0.42 \times $ _____ $ = 4.2$

$0.42 \times 10^2 = $ _____

$0.42 \times 10^3 = $ _____

Solve.

Show your work.

15. The Sunrise Café gets tea bags in boxes of 1,000. If the café charges $1.75 for each cup of tea, and each cup of tea gets one tea bag, how much money does the café receive if they use a whole box of 1,000 teabags?

_____

16. If a box of tea bags costs $95, how much money does the café actually make after they have used up the box of tea and have paid for it?

_____

Remembering

Add or subtract.

1. $10 - 3\frac{3}{4}$

2. $\frac{5}{8} + \frac{3}{8}$

3. $6\frac{4}{5} - 1\frac{1}{5}$

4. $2\frac{1}{3} + 5\frac{1}{3}$

5. $1\frac{2}{9} + 3\frac{5}{9}$

6. $5\frac{1}{2} - \frac{1}{2}$

Copy each exercise. Then add or subtract.

7. $0.67 + 0.42 =$ _____

8. $7 - 3.2 =$ _____

9. $7.8 - 0.8 =$ _____

Solve.

10. $\begin{array}{r} 4.3 \\ \times\ 6.7 \\ \hline \end{array}$

11. $\begin{array}{r} 0.70 \\ \times\ 5.6 \\ \hline \end{array}$

12. $\begin{array}{r} 0.32 \\ \times\ 2.4 \\ \hline \end{array}$

13. **Stretch Your Thinking** Complete the equation $8.9 \cdot \square = 8,900$ using a power of ten. Explain how the product will change if the exponent changes.

_____

_____

_____

_____

Compare Shift Patterns

Homework

Round to the nearesth tenth.

1. 0.38 _____   **2.** 0.94 _____   **3.** 0.621 _____   **4.** 0.087 _____

Round to the nearest hundredth.

5. 0.285 _____   **6.** 0.116 _____   **7.** 0.709 _____   **8.** 0.563 _____

Write an estimated answer for each problem.
Then find and write each exact answer.

Estimated Answer	**Exact Answer**

9. $38 \times 92 \approx$ _____ $\times$ _____ $\approx$ _____ $38 \times 92 =$ _____

10. $8.1 \times 4.2 \approx$ _____ $\times$ _____ $\approx$ _____ $8.1 \times 4.2 =$ _____

11. $7.65 \times 0.9 \approx$ _____ $\times$ _____ $\approx$ _____ $7.65 \times 0.9 =$ _____

12. $3.8 \times 6.02 \approx$ _____ $\times$ _____ $\approx$ _____ $3.8 \times 6.02 =$ _____

13. $1.02 \times 0.9 \approx$ _____ $\times$ _____ $\approx$ _____ $1.02 \times 0.9 =$ _____

Solve.

Show your work.

14. A factory makes 394 motorcycles each week. If there
are 52 weeks in a year, how many motorcycles will the
factory make in a year?

Estimate: _____

Exact answer: _____

15. CDs are $15.25 each. How much will it cost to buy 3?

Estimate: _____

Exact answer: _____

Name _____ **Date** _____

Remembering

Round to the nearest whole number.

1. 5.159 _____

2. 12.7 _____

3. 4.872 _____

Round to the nearest tenth.

4. 45.461 _____

5. 3.12 _____

6. 77.039 _____

Write an equation. Then solve.

Show your work.

7. A rectangle has an area of 48 square feet and a length of 10 feet. What is its width?

_____

8. A length of string that is 22 feet long is being cut into pieces that are $\frac{1}{3}$ foot long. How many pieces will there be?

_____

Solve.

9. $\begin{array}{r} 100 \\ \times\ 3.7 \\ \hline \end{array}$

10. $\begin{array}{r} 5.6 \\ \times\ 0.4 \\ \hline \end{array}$

11. $\begin{array}{r} 0.14 \\ \times\ 60 \\ \hline \end{array}$

12. $\begin{array}{r} 7.1 \\ \times\ 2.9 \\ \hline \end{array}$

13. $\begin{array}{r} 6.8 \\ \times\ 0.5 \\ \hline \end{array}$

14. $\begin{array}{r} 5.8 \\ \times\ 1.2 \\ \hline \end{array}$

15. **Stretch Your Thinking** Taylor estimated the music department would raise $1,100 for new uniforms by selling tickets to a performance next week. Each ticket will be $12.75. About how many tickets does the music department need to sell for Taylor's estimate to be reasonable?

_____

_____

Estimate Products

Name _____ **Date** _____

Homework

Find each product.

1. 57
    $\times 0.31$

2. 0.29
    $\times\ \ 74$

3. 7.6
    $\times\ 8.3$

4. 0.35
    $\times\ \ 94$

5. 4.8
    $\times 0.92$

6. 6.5
    $\times 0.81$

7. 84
    $\times 0.13$

8. 0.9
    $\times 0.04$

Solve. Check that your answers are reasonable.   *Show your work.*

9. Josefina is buying 10 pounds of salmon which costs
   $6.78 per pound. How much will the salmon cost?

   _____

10. It is 9.2 miles between Mr. Rossi's place of work and his
    home. Because he comes home for lunch, he drives this
    distance 4 times a day. How far does Mr. Rossi drive
    each day?

    _____

11. Mr. Rossi works 20 days a month. How far does he drive
    in a month?

    _____

12. Gayle is saving to buy a bicycle. The bicycle costs $119.90.
    She has saved 0.7 of what she needs. How much has
    she saved so far?

    _____

Remembering

Multiply.

1. $98 \cdot 15 =$ _____

2. $658 \cdot 7 =$ _____

3. $54 \cdot 7 =$ _____

4. $3{,}147 \cdot 4 =$ _____

5. $5{,}609 \cdot 2 =$ _____

6. $66 \cdot 75 =$ _____

Write your answers as fractions.

7. $\frac{2}{9} \cdot 5 =$ _____

8. $\frac{3}{4} \cdot 9 =$ _____

9. $\frac{2}{3} \cdot 7 =$ _____

10. $\frac{7}{12} \cdot 15 =$ _____

11. $\frac{5}{8} \cdot 3 =$ _____

12. $\frac{5}{6} \cdot 9 =$ _____

Round to the nearest tenth.

13. 0.43 _____

14. 0.88 _____

15. 0.076 _____

Round to the nearest hundredth.

16. $0.456 =$ _____

17. 0.109 _____

18. $0.541 =$ _____

19. **Stretch Your Thinking** Write a multiplication word problem using decimals for both factors. Then solve your word problem.

_____

_____

_____

_____

Multiplication Practice

Homework

The life cycle of a butterfly has four stages. One stage is a caterpillar

←——————5.2 cm——————→

0.9 cm

Using the length and height of the caterpillar shown, use the descriptions below to draw the adult butterfly that develops from the caterpillar. Remember, a tenth of a centimeter is a millimeter.

▶ The length of your butterfly should be 3.6 times the height of the caterpillar.

▶ The wingspan of your butterfly should be 1.75 times the length of the caterpillar.

Remembering

Write a decimal number for each word name.

1. six hundredths

_____

2. fourteen and eight thousandths

_____

3. nine thousandths

_____

4. five tenths

_____

Solve.

5. $\frac{1}{2} \div 10 =$ _____

6. $\frac{1}{5} \cdot 4 =$ _____

7. $12 \cdot \frac{1}{4} =$ _____

8. $\frac{1}{9} \div 3 =$ _____

9. $\frac{2}{3} \cdot \frac{2}{5} =$ _____

10. $3 \div \frac{1}{6} =$ _____

Find each product.

11. $\begin{array}{r} 0.48 \\ \times 23 \\ \hline \end{array}$

12. $\begin{array}{r} 0.35 \\ \times 13 \\ \hline \end{array}$

13. $\begin{array}{r} 0.86 \\ \times 91 \\ \hline \end{array}$

14. $\begin{array}{r} 0.37 \\ \times 6.5 \\ \hline \end{array}$

15. $\begin{array}{r} 0.22 \\ \times 76 \\ \hline \end{array}$

16. $\begin{array}{r} 5.4 \\ \times 3.2 \\ \hline \end{array}$

17. Stretch Your Thinking Sarah is stringing insect beads to make a bracelet. The butterfly bead is 0.45 inch long and the ladybug bead has a length of 0.27 inch. She uses each type of insect bead and places them end to end. How many of each type of bead does she use to make a line of insect beads measuring 1.71 inches?

_____

Focus on Mathematical Practices